THE SECRET POLITICAL ADVISER

THE SECRET POLITICAL ADVISER

The Unredacted Files of
The Man in the Room Next Door

MICHAEL SPICER

CANONGATE

First published in Great Britain, the USA and Canada in 2020
by Canongate Books Ltd, 14 High Street, Edinburgh EH1 1TE

Distributed in the USA by Publishers Group West and in Canada by
Publishers Group Canada

canongate.co.uk

2

British Library Cataloguing-in-Publication Data
A catalogue record for this book is available on
request from the British Library

ISBN 978 1 83885 314 3

Typeset in Sabon LT Pro by Ed Pickford

Printed and bound in Great Britain by printed and bound in
Great Britain by Clays Ltd, Elcograf S.p.A.

INTRODUCTION

Publisher's Foreword

In July 2020, Canongate came into ownership of a hard drive, sent anonymously to our offices.

The hard drive contained emails, texts, journal entries, social media messages, fragments taken from notebooks, internal memos, phone transcripts and various other pieces of classified intel, all written by the same man over a four-year period. In all correspondence he is known simply as 'M'.

From gathering the information together, we have established that M is the infamous 'Man in the Room Next Door', a special adviser employed by a covert organisation to guide western politicians and other public figures through moments of crisis and upheaval.

After weeks of careful deliberation, we have decided to publish the contents of this hard drive. The material on it refers to events that took place between 2016 and 2020, beginning with the UK EU Referendum result and the rise of President Trump, and ending with the emergence of Covid-19 and the demise of President Trump.

We tried very hard to track M down and to find out more about the organisation he works for, referred to throughout the intel as 'Axworthy'. However, our investigations proved fruitless.

What you are about to read is the truth: the truth behind the most turbulent period of British and American history in more than fifty years. No document has been censored. These are the unredacted files of the Man in the Room Next Door.

AXWORTHY GLOBAL

PO BOX 998 · ALDINGTON ST · KW17 5EH

24 June 2016

The Right Honourable David Cameron
10 Downing Street
Westminster
London SW1A 2AA

Dear David

RE: YOUR RESIGNATION

I am writing this letter with great sadness. Sadness that our working relationship has come to an end and sadness that you were prepared to risk flushing your career down the toilet faster than an exuberant child on a water slide.

Promising to hold an EU Referendum in order to convince a few Eurosceptic, xenophobic knuckleheads to vote Conservative in the 2015 election may, at the time, have seemed like a move of breathtaking genius on your part (after all, you won). But somehow you didn't factor in that you would have to deliver on that promise eventually; it wasn't just some unpaid parking ticket you could squirrel away in the glove compartment with the toffees and tissues.

And now here we are: your legacy is an upturned casserole, seeping into a deep pile carpet, nothing but an irremovable stain by which to remember you. And you have only yourself to blame.

I just had to stop typing briefly to slow handclap you.

During the referendum campaign it was you against former London mayor Boris Johnson, and with whom did the public feel more affinity? Johnson. The very opposite of the people's politician, a catastrophe magnet who can't tie his shoelace without burning down a school. I'm surprised your resignation speech wasn't just a series of sobbing noises in closed brackets.

In the wake of this cataclysmic disaster, my only advice to you is to go as soon as you can. The instigators of the Leave campaign didn't really want this result. They just wanted to fire a warning shot with regards to your premiership, to let you know the vultures were ready to stretch their wings for a little circling in the near future. The mortified faces of Michael Gove and Boris Johnson this afternoon made it abundantly clear that a narrow defeat for them was their ideal outcome. Now they've got a builder's skip of clusterfuck on their gated driveway and no one's going to move it.

Go, and go *now*. Don't even try to make sense of the chaos that will burden the United Kingdom for the next twenty years. Don't even see out the day. Go home and watch *Bargain Hunt*. This action won't save your legacy, because that is beyond the capabilities of any historian: your biography should just be a flip book of a man jumping into a barrel as it rolls off a cliff. However, leaving office with bugger all in place to ensure a smooth transition for your successor is the least you can do to those treacherous mealy-mouthed pufferfish who threw you under the bus.

It won't affect me. I'm planning on taking a sabbatical myself.

Enjoy that caravan you're going to buy. That's all you've got now.

Yours,

M.

Balls. Double balls.

Axworthy have called me in. Seems they've been approached by Theresa May for PPD.* Dear God, no. The very thought of operating the strings of that particular haunted marionette fills me with dread from my toes to my lobes.

They promised me a break. They said once Cameron was gone, they'd promote someone else; give some other poor soul the toxic shit-shovel and hazmat suit. But no.

The overreliance on me is worrying. Axworthy is the most intimidating and fearsome behemoth of an organisation and yet even they can't find anyone else to manage the ceaseless onslaught of political ineptitude in this country.

I am of course flattered by their faith in me, but the fact is, after six years trying to turn David Cameron into a great statesman, I'm a husk. I'm a memory of a husk. The man left his daughter behind in a pub, for God's sake.

I'm going to have to set some ground rules this time. Every time she makes a catastrophic error of judgement, I get the next bank holiday off. Something like that.

* <u>Public Persuasion Duty</u>

From: M [mailto: m@axworthy.com]
Sent: 12th July 2016 06:45
To: no10-communications@gov.org.uk
Subject: PM May's Maiden Speech Notes

Dear All,

Thank you for sending me Prime Minister May's speech ahead of her address this afternoon. It is clear from giving it the once-over that you made the rookie mistake all new speechwriters commit: letting the person reading it out have anything to do with it. Bless you.

But let me remind you that when a toddler asks if they can play with the remote control, you take the batteries out first so they can't do any damage. By all means, let the PM *believe* she's written it, just ensure it is signed off without a single comma in it attributable to her.

I know it sounds like an impossible task but over the years this will become second nature to you. Politicians are not writers. If they were, they wouldn't need writers.

For future reference, always write the PM's speeches when she's not in the same room as you. Keep her at arm's length. Perhaps you should set up your writing room adjacent to a room full of distractions like a fancy Nespresso machine or a half-finished jigsaw of a lovely mountain. Whatever. Just stall her.

Having said that, it's not a bad first attempt. See my notes below:

'In David Cameron I follow in the footsteps of a great modern prime minister.'

Get her to rehearse this line to ensure she can deliver it without smirking.

'. . . fighting against the burning injustice that if you're born poor you will die on average nine years earlier than others.'

I would lose this part. You can't paint yourself as a bastion of social equality arriving to shake things up if you've been at the heart of government since 2010. What has she been doing the last six years if she wasn't fighting burning injustices as Home Secretary? Learning the flute? Making her own plum jam?

'When we take the big calls we will think not of the powerful, but of you. When we pass new laws we will listen not to the mighty, but to you.'

Again, lose this. The general public sees through empty statements. They know the rich and powerful still hold all the cards and that that's why there are more tax loopholes in this country than there are arseholes in Westminster.

That should do for now. No point burdening you with heavy notes for a maiden speech: they're famously scant on detail and you don't want to defy decades of tradition by making the PM say anything significant.

Best of luck,

M.

Monday 2 August 2016 10.15

M, I need to talk to you urgently.

Can it wait? I'm trying to make
Theresa May seem human and it's
draining all my energy.

As you know, Axworthy dispatched
me to Hollywood last summer.

Oh, I am pleased. Do go on. How's
the weather over there? How juicy are
the oranges? How beautiful are the
people? Does everyone look like Chris
Hemsworth and Olivia Wilde? When
was the last time you saw a thick
sheet of miserable low cloud?

I've just been contacted by Clint
Eastwood's PR team. They want
me to be in his ear when he
conducts a series of interviews to
promote his next film.

Why?

Because in recent weeks he's been defending presidential candidate Donald Trump for making racist remarks.

Oh.

Eastwood believes Trump is heroically railing against political correctness.

Oh good. That's just what we need. More white guys using offensive language to describe how they can't use offensive language any more.

How am I supposed to convince Clint Eastwood that he should take direction from me? He's the epitome of staunchness. Plus I'm pretty sure he's 95% granite now. I need help here. What am I going to do?

Well, Eastwood is the embodiment of 20th century masculinity: to many white men who see him as a beacon of traditional American values, it's comforting to read a magazine interview where he snaps and grizzles about 'the endangered white man'. It won't change anything, so where's the harm? He reminds me of my potty uncle who thinks onions are getting a bit too 'mosque-shaped' these days. Tell his team not to worry: his career will survive.

They don't care about his career. They believe these interviews could be the turning point, that he could crystallise the argument between progressives and those who want to get back to when men were men, back to the good old days of traditional family values and polio. They think his words could chime with swathes of Republicans who may well vote Trump into the White House this November.

Oh please. Trump? It's been a tremendously surreal ride with the silly old bag of flour, but I think the White House is one uneconomical luxury accommodation he WON'T be able to get his hands on.

You sound terribly sure of yourself.

I'm just feeling lucky. 'I'm feeling lucky, punk!'

That's not what he says.

Oh.

Diary: Wednesday 10th August 2016

Woken at two a.m. by our man in Washington.
It seems Trump has said if Hillary Clinton becomes
president and gets to pick her judges there will be
nothing the American public can do about her taking
away the second amendment; then hinted to those
who carry arms that there is one other way.

So he essentially joked that she should be shot.
Luckily the United States doesn't have a strong
historical association with assassinated leaders, so
this is fine.

Axworthy are becoming increasingly concerned
that if Trump does become POTUS, and therefore
automatically our client, we'll be working tirelessly
around the clock, pouring all our resources into this
dangerously inept plum cake and putting too much
strain on the already stretched team.

With that in mind, I may suggest to the top brass that – for the first time in fifty years – the Axworthy organisation retracts its longstanding services to the presidency. I imagine that'll go down about as well as when I suggested a birthday cake ban in the office.*

* There are just too many February birthdays. By the beginning of March my blood type is Colin the Caterpillar.

NOTES

IDEAS FOR NON-CONTROVERSIAL / NEUTRAL / UNINTERESTING / DULL HOLIDAY DESTINATIONS FOR PM MAY

<u>Nowhere in the EU</u> - The severity of pro-Leave zealotry in the country right now would mean those beetroots interpreting any jaunt across the Channel as something akin to urinating against the White Cliffs of Dover whilst dressed as a baguette. Which would at least be a cheaper excursion to arrange.

<u>Tulum, Mexico</u> - Instagram influencers are flocking here for the interesting architecture, gorgeous coast and vegan food, which could give the PM some cred. The only drawback is her presence could automatically suck all the cred out of Tulum, so by the time she left the place, it would have the same appeal as Tamworth.

<u>Canary Islands</u> - Despite being in the EU, Spanish islands are always a good bet; Brits see

them as a kind of hot Southend. I'm sure a lot of Brexiteers think we own them. The problem with this option is the PM would have to hide her disdain for the other Brits holidaying out there too. And generally speaking, her disdain-hiding abilities are woeful: looks like a cat in its basket on the way to the vet's.

The Swiss Alps – She's always banging on about her love for hiking so this could be a warmly-welcomed suggestion. We could take photos of her looking relaxed, wearing sunglasses, smiling, enjoying life, leaning on a Nordic pole and staring off into the distance, thinking about stricter prison reforms.

Disneyland, Paris – Strictly speaking this is in the EU, but Disneyland is great for pun-laden puff pieces. 'PM Vows Not to Take the Mickey When It Comes to the Brexit Withdrawal Agreement', '"I Won't Make Any Goofs on the Intervention in Yemen," says PM After Hair-Raising Teacup Ride', 'When It Comes to Border Controls, I Haven't Gone Jafar Enough', etc.

<u>Devon or Cornwall</u> – Plenty of Tory voters, lots of places to have a cream tea and two of the few regions in the UK that will make her look positively dynamic.

<u>Dubai</u> – Cons: built by modern-day slavery. Pros: lovely aquarium.

<u>USA</u> – A brief informal visit to see Hillary might help establish a much-needed diplomatic bond ahead of her election win.

<u>Oxfordshire</u> – I'd like to send the PM to a sleepy Oxfordshire village for a week on the off-chance that the murder of a wealthy local developer takes place at the same time. I just think she'd make a good TV detective. Philip as her trusty sidekick... Maybe there could be a series: 'The Hiking Detective'? That could be her thing. Like Sherlock Holmes and his violin. OK, yes, I'm bored of this list now.

From: Martin Doherty [mailto: martindoherty@axworthy.com]
Sent: 25th August 2016 10:23
To: M [mailto: m@axworthy.com]
Subject: Farageband

Hello M,

How's the Westminster turd-polishing business?

Just thought I should touch base with you re this Nigel Farage. He's on our radar today because he's in Mississippi with Trump for one of his cheering-and-balloon extravaganzas. Have you ever been to one of these? It's essentially an 8-year-old's birthday party but much, much larger. And where the 8-year-old is also the hired clown.

Anyway, the file on Farage here in the US is as old as his dress sense. We need some fresh data on him before the rally. Axworthy are keen for us to monitor his and Trump's relationship in case DJT is elected in November. It's almost as if our superiors know something we don't.

Please could you provide a quick doc of any info that could be useful? We know that he's a divisive political figure in the United Kingdom and we also know that it's impossible to gauge where his neck ends and his head begins but that's about it.

Look forward to hearing from you.

Marty

From: M [mailto: m@axworthy.com]
Sent: 25th August 2016 10:51
To: Martin Doherty [mailto: martindoherty@axworthy.com]
Subject: Farageband

Dear McFly,

Thanks for your email.

I have attached a quick fact file on Farage, though quite why Axworthy thinks their relationship is worth monitoring is beyond me. Trump has obviously been advised by his cabal of degenerate carpet sharks that associating with the current leading light in modern British bigotry will help globalise his campaign and, crucially, galvanise anti-liberal feeling across the west.

But let's be in no doubt: this fling is for one night only. The frothy-mouthed, corduroy-cap-wearing *Dad's Army* caricature will no doubt enjoy watching his divisive rhetoric being hoovered up by Trump's hardcore army tonight, but trust me, as soon as Farage has endorsed Trump, the honeymoon will be over. It'll be 'Back to Sevenoaks with you and make your own way to the airport, puddle-mouth'.

Farage to Trump is just a doorman. And once he's opened that door, Farage is expendable. He's just a man. Standing alone by a door. Wearing a silly hat.

But who am I to argue against the strategies of our superiors? Hope the file is more use than the man himself.

Best,

M.

Thursday 25th August 2016

Nigel Farage – What to Know

Frankly, the less you know about him the better: it's like asking for a fact file on warts or poisonous insects. Who really wants to know? What follows are a few pointers. If you need anything else, God forbid, let me know.

Farage and UKIP

Farage has an odd relationship with his own party. As leader he clearly possessed lofty ambitions for its development and future but, regrettably for him, the extraordinary way in which the party attracted the country's most dangerously ignorant, jingoistic dimwits meant that, on the face of it, UKIP would always come across as rather pantomimic. Less mainstream political party, more Mad Hatter's Tea Party.

When Farage tried resigning in 2015, the party refused to accept his resignation because they knew without him at the helm throwing his weight around in Europe (and appearing on BBC's *Question Time* more often than the theme tune) the curtain would well and truly be ripped away, exposing UKIP as the wildly ineffectual, tinpot rabble of blustering lunatics we always suspected it to be.

Farage and Europe

He savours every moment in the European Parliament – not because his supporters back home see him as a modern British crusader against European federalism, but because he enjoys being a nuisance. And that's what puts the sugar in his tea: being loathed. This is because loathing leads to rage, rage leads to fighting and fighting leads to discord, political splits, divisive rhetoric and extreme policies. A four-course meal made in heaven, for Nige.

You only have to look at his boiled face to know what motivates him. He's like Dennis Hopper in *Blue Velvet*, only the gas in the tank is continental disdain.

Farage and the US

We understand Farage has close links with Trump's chief strategist and part-time offal impersonator Steve Bannon. One can only imagine what the discourse is like:

'So our team in the US is gonna create political intolerance throughout the western world via a highly sophisticated campaign of Russian-backed social media infiltration.'

'Righty-o.'

'What about you?'

'I'm going to complain to the BBC for editing racial colloquialisms out of old sitcoms.'

'Sorry, what?'

Farage and the Environment

Farage doesn't have time for climate change. Not yet anyway. When he's hurriedly adapting his Range Rover Discovery into an amphibious 4x4 and propelling himself into town for marked-up lifejackets from House of Fraser, *then* he'll have time for it. But at the moment he's one of those rah-rah-pish-and-nonsense puffins who believe the green agenda to reverse the damage done to the world is nothing but a liberal scam. Quite how saving the planet can be interpreted as some sort of hoax is a theory I've yet to fully comprehend.

Farage and Smoking

Farage was against the public smoking ban and saw his own habit as an act of solidarity and defiance. This is the kind of man you're dealing with: someone who smokes a cigarette indoors and thinks they're Thomas Becket.

Miscellaneous Farage Data I've Made Up That Might Not Be True But Probably Is

1) He has a glass-fronted cabinet in the living room full of dubious-looking porcelain figurines.

2) He has a functioning VHS recorder.

3) He has an ornately framed oil painting of a horse and cart on the wall above his bed.

4) He never makes eye contact with anyone who works in a coffee shop.

5) Whenever he smells a barbecue in his neighbourhood, he calls the police.

6) He never shares a sharing bag of chocolates.

7) Whenever he witnesses someone breast-feeding in public, he calls the police.

8) He never asks where the toilets are in a restaurant, believing it to be a sign of weakness.

9) He has never ridden a pedalo.

10) He smells all fruit with suspicion before putting it in his shopping basket.

11) He has a wavy front-garden hedge of which he is overly proud.

12) When he has a builder in his house, he calls him 'matey'.

13) He has a Tower of London Beefeater costume he puts on when he's alone and sad.

14) His computer has a maximum-sized cursor that takes up a quarter of the screen.

15) He doesn't understand the system at Argos.

16) He once sat in the children's sandpit in a recreational park for forty minutes talking about border controls to a sock puppet on his hand.

17) He doesn't cook very often, but when he does, he wears an apron with a tea towel over the shoulder and he says 'make room make room make room' when he takes something out of the oven.

18) He will press the button on the pedestrian crossing a little bit harder than you just to make sure.

19) He has a little stool in his garage for cleaning the roof of his car.

20) A little fucking stool. You know he does.

Day off today. It's a welcome break. Axworthy and Downing Street are having a spat over an 'access to Theresa May' lunch being held during the Conservative Party conference next month. The idea is that if corporate execs are willing to stump up £3,000, they can attend a lunch with the Prime Minister and assorted cabinet members.

Quite why anyone would want access to Theresa May is confusing to begin with. Two hours in the company of her and her colleagues and you'd be paying to be removed from the table. Perhaps I should provide that as a service? 'Engaged in a torturous lunch with the leader of this country? For £3,000 I can kidnap you and transfer you to the cloakroom with a bag of crisps and a fizzy drink until she's gone.'

Axworthy believe this lunch to be an open goal for the media and have ordered me to stand down until the matter is resolved, which I fully expect it to be.

Someone sent me the provisional itinerary for the lunch and it's pretty clear from the way it scans that Downing Street need us more than we need them.

12.00: Introduction by Philip Hammond (crispy squid)

12.25: Protecting jobs with Dominic Raab (compressed watermelon)

12.50: Modernising the economy with Michael Gove (roasted squab pigeon)

13.15: Regional productivity with Matt Hancock and Liam Fox (smoked duck and caramelised peach)

13.45: The business sector with Damian Green (baked aubergine)

14.10: The future of housing with Liz Truss (torched halibut)

14.30: The importance of local community with Prime Minister May (apricot jelly)

AXWORTHY GLOBAL

PO BOX 998 · ALDINGTON ST · KW17 5EH

From: M

To: Dipak and Charlotte

Date: 21/09/16

Heading: PP Dalton

Message:

I'm as surprised as you are. As we have always made clear, Axworthy is apolitical. We are a hired gun. No more, no less. Nevertheless, my jaw was firmly caked in porridge this morning when I got the email saying Jeremy Corbyn requires our assistance.

It seems he is at the end of his tether with regards to the outspoken author PP Dalton, famous for her series of renowned children's sci-fi books about a time-travelling boy called Wayne Harmony.

According to Mr Corbyn and his advisers, the ceaseless call-to-arms by Ms Dalton to form a new breakaway party is too much of a distraction, and they have asked us to do something about it. Something entirely legal but at the same time entirely damaging.

In case you're not up to speed with Ms Dalton's Twitter feed, here are a few choice tweets relating to the matter. Once you've digested these, let's arrange a meeting ASAP and see what we can come up with.

PP Dalton @MsPPDalton · Jan 9

Brexit is the fault of Corbyn. If he'd campaigned for Remain instead of posting pics from his allotment of his favourite marrow we wouldn't be in this mess.

PP Dalton @MsPPDalton · Jan 25

Survey shows Corbyn is seen as more 'in touch' with people than Boris Johnson. So? The golden armour of Henry II of France is more in touch than Boris Johnson. Enough Corbyn-cuddling. He needs to go!

PP Dalton @MsPPDalton · Feb 2

I'm backing Owen Smith for the Labour leadership. He looks like the sort of person who'd bore you rigid about a recent cycling weekend he'd been on with his friend Ian [1/2]

but he's got my vote because his message is clear – he isn't and never has been Jeremy Corbyn. [2/2]

PP Dalton @MsPPDalton · Feb 15

We need a *real* leader. Big news on its way!

PP Dalton @MsPPDalton · Feb 27

We cannot carry on with Corbyn at the helm. And so it is with a heavy heart that I announce I am renouncing my membership of the Labour Party. [1/2]

I'm joining my friends in a new breakaway party campaigning for a different EU referendum. We're called the Differeferendum Party. Join us! [2/2]

PP Dalton @MsPPDalton · Mar 3

It is with a heavy heart that I announce I am leaving the Differeferendum Party due to differences over the different referendum. The only way we can beat Corbyn is if we work together. [1/2]

If anyone has any ideas for a new party, please leave a message with my agent Trinny. [2/2]

PP Dalton @MsPPDalton · Mar 15

Pleased to be offering my support this morning to the new Central Democratic UK Freedom Party. This is a game changer! Corbyn out!

PP Dalton @MsPPDalton · Mar 21

The Central Democratic UK Freedom Party is now defunct. But don't fear! The best minds from the CDUKFP and the Differeferendum Party are coming together. [1/2]

They'll form a lasting challenger to Corbyn's brand of harmful far-left politics. They don't have a name yet but I'm sure it will be a good one. [2/2]

PP Dalton @MsPPDalton · Apr 3

Just been to my first meeting with the Centralist Democrats for Real Change Party and I don't think I'm exaggerating when I say Corbyn will be dust in a matter of months.

PP Dalton @MsPPDalton · Apr 4

It is with a heavy heart that I announce that the Centralist Democrats for Real Change Party appears to have disbanded. Or at least, he's not returning my calls. More news as I get it.

PP Dalton @MsPPDalton · Apr 25

Sorry to say that the Centralist Democrats for Real Change Party has joined the Lib Dems. The idiot.

PP Dalton @MsPPDalton · May 1

OK, this is it now. For the first time in months, I'm sensing hope. Please click on the link to become a member of the Kingdom United Party. www.kup.com/join [1/2]

This is different. Together we will defeat Corbyn and ditch the Tories with one movement. Definitely this time. #UpForTheKup [2/2]

22 September 2016 07.34

Morning, any thoughts re: PP?

M @

This KUP is certainly gaining momentum. Looks worrying for Corbyn. I can see why his people contacted us.

Dipak @

9 MPs defected this morning. It's really bad for Labour. We need to put something out this afternoon if we're going to do anything.

Charlotte @

Quite, so what have we got?

M @

We need to take PP out of the picture. PP is the culprit. The whole movement will fizzle out if she's gone.

Dipak @

Our people on the inside have confirmed the only reason she is so invested in removing Corbyn is because she's supposed to be writing a book and is looking for anything to distract her from actually doing it. At the beginning of the year she had a play to write so she started a campaign to get her local council to put locks on wheelie bins to deter foxes.

Charlotte @

Great, so how do we take her out of the picture legally? Do we have any dirt on her?

M @

I don't think it's a case of needing significant dirt, I think it's more about getting to her psychologically, so she takes HERSELF out of the picture.

Dipak @

I like that thinking. Example?

M @

She's fragile; her feathers are easily ruffled. If you reveal anything she might see as bad for her image – ideally anything that goes against her working-class, woman-of-the-people image – however minor, it would just grow and grow and grow in her mind until she couldn't think of anything else. And then boom . . . No more KUP.

Charlotte @

Right, so we need a tiny detail about her to leak to the media. Any ideas?

M @

Well, the refuse collectors on her route loathe her because each of them now has to wear a belt with a massive bunch of wheelie bin keys as big as beach balls. Several employees have already taken sick days for hernia-related injuries. We could talk to one of them?

Dipak @

That's good but I'm thinking of something more personal. Something that will burrow away at her psyche.

M @

There's an apocryphal story that she once made a waiter throw away a bowl of pasta because he shredded Parmesan over the meal and she wanted it grated.

Charlotte @

Bingo.

M @

WHAT A MISTAKE-A TO MAKE-A!

Wayne Harmony author throws hissy fit in Italian restaurant following harmesan to her Parmesan

It has been revealed that PP Dalston, one of the most famous children's authors in the world, last month had a tantrum in a North London restaurant after a waiter shredded Parmesan over her meal instead of grating it.

The 55-year-old author responsible for the iconic series of books about a 10-year-old time-traveller was seen lashing out at the waiter after he used the larger holes of a cheese grater to shred Parmesan over her meal rather than her preferred method of sprinkling finely grated cheese over it via a spoon.

According to nearby diners, Ms Dalston – whose private wealth is reported to be around £500 million – grabbed the waiter's wrist as he started to shred the Parmesan and bellowed, 'What on earth do you think you're doing?' When the waiter explained that he was shredding Parmesan over her meal, Ms Dalston erupted and exclaimed, 'You don't shred thick strips of Parmesan over pasta like that – you grate it finely in the kitchen and bring it out here with a bowl and a spoon for me to sprinkle on myself.'

Robert Jennings @RobertJenningsEsq

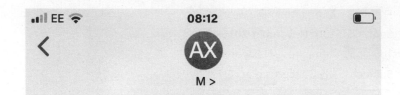
1 October 2016 08.04

Well done, everyone.

Robert Jennings
@RobertJenningsEsq · Oct 1
The Kingdom United Party is over. No official reason given but its benefactor PP Dalston is said to have jetted to the Maldives this a.m. after #Grategate.

M @

Hello A,

As requested, I'm currently in the departure lounge at Gatwick, bound for Washington DC. My flight is inevitably delayed so instead of spending hundreds of pounds in Cath Kidston – my preferred pursuit when I need to pass the time in this godforsaken aeronautical shitscape – I have decided to sit and write this email to you, regarding the representation of the 45th President of the United States.

I do not want us to represent the 45th President of the United States.

I understand from DC HQ that the wheels are already in motion and I just want to make it clear from the off that I think it's a very, very, very bad idea. The next four years are going to be bleak, frightening, horrific, depressing and yet somehow utterly predictable too: it's going to be a four-year-long M. Night Shyamalan film. Please reconsider.

Ever since the organisation was first brought over from the UK to assist President Ford in the aftermath of Watergate, we have remained by the side of the commander-in-chief. With varying degrees of success, admittedly, but we have done it without anyone knowing we exist and therefore with our credibility intact. I fear this period of stability will unravel with the next president.

As your most senior adviser, I predict without hesitation that President Trump will be impossible to counsel. He will ignore our guidance and over time will tarnish our reputation inside government circles. He will wear us down until we're nothing more than a local outfit doing quick surveillance jobs from a Citroën Berlingo. In fact, judging by the intel we have on him, I'd say he'll probably try and pull the trigger first (hopefully not literally).

And finally, on a personal note, if we do have to work with him, please don't put me in charge of operations. I have high blood pressure these days and by all accounts working for that man is like working with a klaxon wearing a tie.

Got to go: I've just seen a mustard-coloured notepad in the window of Cath Kidston that is both very expensive and wholly unnecessary, so I'm going to buy five.

Best,

M.

Monday 11 November 2016 02.07

> Can you tell Obama to loosen up just a touch? He looks so rigid having to sit next to Trump.

Listen, M, I respect you, but can you not text me when I'm in the President's ear? Remember this is still my job till the end of the year.

> Sorry it's just, well, look at him . . . He's so uncomfortable, he's on the brink of turning into a hat stand.

Where are you?

> I'm in a cab, leaving Reagan Airport. Watching the feed on my phone.

Wow, you're keen.

No, I am not keen. I have never been LESS keen. Axworthy wanted me here as soon as the result came through. Trump's people have told them they want the narrative controlled ASAP. There are a lot of angry voters out there.

There are a lot of angry voters in here.

And right now Trump is shaking hands with the angriest one of all. Look at him. He's simmering like a boiled egg. You've got to tell him to smile, relax his shoulders, stroke his chin, something, anything. He's got to stop looking at Trump like he wants to smear him in chum and lower him into the North Atlantic Ocean.

I don't have time for this.

I did advise Obama in his first term, you know.

You don't let me forget. Darting between the UK and the US for so many years. I don't know how you did it.

Nor do I.

Well, you're going to have to remember soon, because if you're coming back to advise the top man again, you've only got two months.

You don't seem particularly put out that you're being demoted to make way for me.

It's not a demotion, it's a sideways move. I'm advising the Prime Minister of Australia next year. He's just as important a figure on the international stage.

Who IS the Prime Minister of Australia?

You got me there.

15 November 2016 12.34

> Nikki, are you there? We need to talk.

Yes we do. You have a gazillion messages. You need to get back to the office. Where are you?

> I'm still in Washington. It's the middle of the night. I'm over at the Clintons' place for a nightcap. Hillary's gone to bed. Bill has just passed out next to me on the sofa.

Sorry, what?

> His fluffy, cloud-haired head is drooping and he's still holding an unfinished scotch. He has a snore like a heavy-duty zip.

OK.

He called me over this evening because he wants my advice. You know he has this digital archive freely available to the public online? He wants to publish some redacted phone conversations between himself and Tony Blair.

Oh my God. Are they explosive?

About as explosive as a scented candle. They're exceptionally mundane. So I need you to call Blair's people and find out if TB is OK with these being published online. He doesn't come across badly, but he doesn't come across as the dynamic young leader we worked hard to portray him as either . . . More like a flannel.

OK, roger that. Send over the transcripts and I'll let you know.

Thanks. I've got to go, Bill is inclining towards me at an alarming rate.

MEMORANDUM OF TELEPHONE CONVERSATION

DATE: September 1, 1997

<u>Prime Minister Blair:</u> It's a new initiative,
which we hope will bring unemployment down.

<u>The President:</u> That sounds great. You know we
had a nationwide competition here for unemployed
folk? The prize was one hour in my personal
bowling alley.

<u>Prime Minister Blair:</u> I didn't know that.

<u>The President:</u> This guy from Utah won. Boy,
could he bowl. I never got a sniff of winning a
game.

<u>Prime Minister Blair:</u> I see.

<u>The President:</u> He was rubbing my face in it
by the end. I told him, 'I just authorised a
bombing campaign in Yugoslavia, buddy. Cut it
out.' But he just kept on. Doing these little
dances after each strike. Asshole.

<u>Prime Minister Blair:</u> It must be late where you
are.

DATE: October 12, 1997

<u>Prime Minister Blair:</u> Then of course there's the
issue with tuition fees. I'm very much spinning
plates at the moment.

The President: Have you ever actually done that?

Prime Minister Blair: Done what?

The President: Spun plates?

Prime Minister Blair: Er, no.

The President: I did it once. It was during the '94 midterms. They put on a big rally in Kentucky. I managed sixteen plates.

Prime Minister Blair: That's . . . good.

The President: Sixteen.

Prime Minister Blair: Yes. Well done.

The President: The guy in charge of the plates said it was amazing for a first try.

Prime Minister Blair: How did the Iraq briefing go?

DATE: March 1, 1998

Prime Minister Blair: Bill.

The President: Good afternoon, Prime Minister.

Prime Minister Blair: How are you?

The President: My hands are a little sore today but I'm good.

Prime Minister Blair: Your hands?

The President: Yeah, I punched a ham.

Prime Minister Blair: Sorry, did you say ham?

The President: Yes. I beat this ham to pieces. I do it all the time. Al put me onto it. It expels a lot of frustration, you know? Pent-up stuff. You feel like a king afterwards.

Prime Minister Blair: Oh right.

The President: But you certainly feel it the morning after. Next time I'm over I'll bring a ham. We'll punch it together.

Prime Minister Blair: We have ham here.

DATE: April 25, 1998

Prime Minister Blair: Yes, Bill, nice to hear from you.

The President: I apologise for calling you so late in the evening.

Prime Minister Blair: That's quite all right. Cherie and I are driving back from a charity function in Leeds.

Prime Minister Blair: I love Leeds. Leeds Castle is so beautiful.

Prime Minister Blair: Leeds Castle is in Kent, Bill.

The President: Why is Leeds Castle in Kent?

Prime Minister Blair: I don't know.

The President: Is there a Kent Castle in Leeds?

Prime Minister Blair: No.

The President: If I were in Leeds, I'd be pissed off that Kent has my castle.

Prime Minister Blair: Right.

The President: We don't really have castles here. Not proper castles. The castle in Disneyland is impressive.

Prime Minister Blair: Yes, yes it is. I took the family there two years ago. It's a fantastic castle.

The President: Yes, but compared to UK castles, it's a beer crate. A beer crate full of shit.

Prime Minister Blair: What were you calling about?

The President: I can't remember.

DATE: June 8, 1998

The President: Before I go, could you settle an argument?

Prime Minister Blair: I'll try.

The President: It's B, L, A, R, E, right?

Prime Minister Blair: Sorry?

The President: B, L, A, R—

Prime Minister Blair: Are you talking about my name?

The President: Yeah. It's B, L, A, R, E, yes?

Prime Minister Blair: Are you joking? Is this a joke?

The President: No, I've just been talking to Leon and he said—

Prime Minister Blair: Bill, I am about to do PMQs, can I call you back?

The President: If you would. I've got five bucks riding on this.

Prime Minister Blair: Goodbye, Bill.

The President: How long will you be?

Prime Minister Blair: Hard to say.

The President: OK, I'll go punch a ham until you're done.

Diary: Wednesday 30th November 2016

Heading back home.

Downing Street wants me to take a detour to Serbia to – and I quote – 'seal Boris Johnson's useless carcass inside a massive jiffy bag and post him to the Faroe Islands'.

Apparently he's been promoting his new book about Churchill during an official state visit; signing copies in a book shop.

It's not like alarm bells weren't ringing when he was appointed Foreign Secretary. As Theresa May was assembling her first cabinet – presumably without the instruction manual – the shrill of an old school alarm bell was really all one could hear along the corridors of Westminster. And it sounded peculiarly like 'P-l-e-e-e-e-a-s-s-e n-o-t J-o-h-n-s-o-n... P-l-e-e-e-e-a-s-s-e n-o-t J-o-h-n-s-o-n'.

But that's government for you. As soon as they disappear behind that big black door, they become immune to the sounds outside, most notably the sound of common sense. You don't appoint a character like Boris Johnson to the role of Foreign Secretary. You just don't do that. Not unless you've had a 'Trading Places' -style wager with a colleague that you could turn Great Britain into a bankrupt rock within a year using only the international diplomacy of the nation's favourite rinky-dink posho.

I fear for this government. No, I fear for this country. Anyone can see that Johnson is eyeing up the big prize. He's only a few stepping stones away. I only hope he skips the Chancellor's job otherwise we'll all be in barrels with braces before budget day.

I really must be out of here before he ever becomes PM. I want an allotment. I've decided. I want to grow vegetables in an allotment by the time he clumps into No. 10 like Herman Munster. I must be done with all this by then. I must.

AXWORTHY GLOBAL

PO BOX 998 · ALDINGTON ST · KW17 5EH

From: M

To: All @ Axworthy

Date: 16/12/16

Heading: How to Turn a Watergate into Insignifigate

Message:

It's transition time again, ladies and gentlemen, and as we all know, these periods of political upheaval must be dealt with as smoothly as possible. We are still in the employment of the Obama Administration, and yet we need to prepare for the arrival next month of President Donald J. Trump, our newest client.

Press secretary Josh Earnest has ensured that this transition will be as delicate as a tool bag in a tumble dryer by sharing the views of US intelligence officials that President Putin had a direct role in hacking during the election.

Whether or not these allegations are true, we must not let them cloud our new client's first few months in office. Remember, we are not investigative journalists: we are paid advisers. None of us are Woodward and Bernstein. We're Cyrano de Bergerac with a dash of Winston Wolfe. Never forget that.

So I'm calling on you all to work together to nullify this story by turning it into an irrelevance. And the best way to do that is to confuse the general public.

For example, you could use an argument such as this:

'If a major covert hacking operation was being orchestrated by the world's most sophisticated intelligence service, why have they installed as president the biggest, loudest clodpole in America? A man who literally said "Russia, if you're listening, I hope you're able to find the 30,000 emails that are missing."

Why would you plan years and years of top-level international cyber-espionage and then pick as your president someone who doesn't have an internal edit button? Who spews out whatever he wants, like an erratic vending machine? He's the antithesis of a slick Russian security operation. It doesn't make any sense.

It doesn't make any sense.

It *doesn't* make *any* sense.

Therefore . . .

Let's give him the benefit of the doubt!'

That's the conclusion we have to steer the public towards: if Russia is really trying to dictate international affairs through a pawn in the Oval Office, surely they would have picked a better, more useful pawn? Not a pawn that thinks it's a king; not a pawn that believes it owns the chess board and the box it came in; not a pawn flummoxed by the rules of chess and which would rather be the wishbone in a game of Operation.

If you have any new and interesting ways we can throw the media and the public in general off the scent, please do not hesitate to get in touch. Every time a new road appears leading to Trump in this scandal, it's imperative we stick a lollipop lady across it. A devious, timewasting lollipop lady.

We need to nip this in the bud before the inauguration – which must also go ahead without a hitch, but that's for another day.

I look forward to hearing from you all.

Best,

M.

From: M [mailto: m@axworthy.com]
Sent: 10th January 2017 05:13
To: Jared Kushner
Subject: Notes on your appointment as adviser to the President

Just heard the news, JK. Welcome.

OK, that's the pleasantry out the way. Here are my notes:

- You have been appointed adviser and that must be smashing for you, but on no account must you advise the President without our approval. I don't care if you're his son-in-law. I wouldn't care if you were both Don Jnr AND Eric melded together like Frankenstein's Doofus: you will not go rogue while we're on the scene.

- Please be aware that on the odd occasion you say something to President Trump, we will advise that he forgets it almost instantly, as if it were the last item on a shopping list. In fact, it might be better all-round if you limited your role in the White House to 'human shopping list'. Tell him when the freezer's out of waffles, that sort of thing. We'd be OK with that.

- Your first duty is to make clear that your appointment has nothing to do with the fact that your father-in-law is the commander-in-chief and therefore doesn't break the federal anti-nepotism law. Now, the only way to get round this is to get your father-in-law to change the federal anti-nepotism law. Technically speaking, this is also nepotism but if the law is changed it won't matter.

- Forego any salary during your time in office. Make it seem like you're supporting your father-in-law out of the kindness of your heart. No, wait. First make it seem like you're capable of kindness. No. First make it seem like you have a heart. Like, an actual heart that beats in your chest, rather than a toxic avocado or whatever it is you've got in there.

- If you're required to make financial disclosures, remember not to put too much emphasis on all the foreign investment your company needs – and the extra foreign investment it would undoubtedly receive if you started gallivanting around the world in Air Force One with Pop-Pop. Pretend you're scaling back your operations. Pretend you want to diversify into domestic markets and that global trade is not really your bag any more. Perhaps you've lost all commercial ambition now and just want to become an ice cream man or a Pilates instructor? Get creative!

Finally, POTUS tells me you could be crucial to any future peace talks in the Middle East. Without wishing to sound like one of these old stuffed shirts who are averse to new faces and new ideas, the very notion that you could be sat at a table with foreign ministers discussing the finer points of a 70-years-long conflict that is steeped in religious, ethnic and historical tribulations, when the extent of your knowledge in this field is that you once watched *You Don't Mess with the Zohan* on a long-haul flight, is very worrying. My apologies for my lack of enthusiasm but this is something we'll need to discuss when I'm back in Washington. In the meantime, please stay seated at the children's table.

Signing off for now. See you at the inauguration. Please do nothing till then.

M

From: M [mailto: m@axworthy.com]
Sent: 20th January 2017 04:32
To: C Team [mailto: communications@whitehouse.gov.us]
Subject: Inauguration speech

Dear all,

Apologies for the delay on this, jetlag has rendered me unable to focus or concentrate for any length of time. However, as your country has just elected a man who can't do either of those two things when fully unimpeded by jetlag, I'd say we're on a level playing field.

Here are the key points you need to address in his inauguration speech today (I can't quite believe I just typed that. Donald Trump's inauguration speech. Still doesn't seem real, does it? It's going to feel like watching the Nobel Prize for Literature being presented to the team who came up with 'Baby Shark'):

1. **Law and order:** Talk about crime but don't lay it on too thick. People don't want to be left feeling pessimistic on inauguration day. Tell him not to go off-piste and please refrain from painting pictures of America being some sort of gangland dystopia, similar to *Mad Max* or that part in *Back to the Future Part II* when Biff is rich. Oh wait, that whole segment is about Trump, isn't it? I just realised. Don't tell him.

    Make it clear that he will address a justice system that still treats black people more harshly than white. Maybe get him to ask if anyone in the crowd knows a black person, could they pass on the message.

2. **Reaching out:** Trump has to continue the narrative of putting 'America First', to be the voice of the everyday American in the face of oppression and elitism. He also needs to keep convincing

the American people that he isn't the face of oppression and elitism. He may look remarkably *like* that face – a cousin or uncle, maybe – but it's definitely not him. When it comes to championing the man on the street, Mr President will be sure to gesture a fist of solidarity from his literal gold penthouse apartment balcony.

3. **Allies:** Refer to close alliances with major foreign powers but crucially DO NOT MENTION RUSSIA. There's enough shit flying around right now with regards to cyber-hacking without President Piss-Tape throwing the media a juicy bone on today of all days.

4. **Terrorism:** Don't mention terrorism. Sometimes he gets so riled up, he stops reading the teleprompter. And that's when the embryonic ideas tumble out of his mouth like coins from a slot machine. Seriously. The absolute hell-pits of his abandoned fairground of a brain get to work during these moments. If we can make absolutely sure he doesn't accidentally start a war on that podium today, that would be super.

5. **Healthcare:** I notice from early drafts of this speech that POTUS aims to 'free the Earth from the miseries of disease'. Any chance you could take this sentence out? Here's the reason why it's a little problematic: it makes absolutely no fucking sense at all. None. Healthcare in America is a scandal and the only thing he has to say about it in his inauguration speech is that he will cure the world? The whole world? That's not even false prophet territory, that's the sort of insanity you'd see written in shit on the wall of a maximum-security prison. Please kindly omit.

6. **Immigration:** Leave out any mention of borders as it inevitably stirs up 'them and us' animosity which, again, you simply don't do during an inauguration speech. That includes any mention of his wall. I know he's very proud of his plan for a big wall – I bet

he spent a long time sat on the floor with a pot of pens, drawing it and colouring it in – but today is not the day to hold it up to the crowd and say 'wall keep the bad out'.

7. **Climate:** I see nothing in here about climate change either. Now this hasn't come as any surprise to me because a) 45 has ties to fossil fuel companies and b) his brain is incapable of making the distinction between the weather and climate. ('How can global warming be a thing when it's snowing in the rose garden?', etc.)

However, I would advise inserting a small, ambiguous line in the speech, perhaps about clean oceans – anything that placates the green activists yet is vague enough not to provoke the fossil fuel sector or the generic Trump conspiracy theorist who thinks the wind turbine is a giant piece of Democrat-funded, brainwashing apparatus designed to hypnotise all patriotic alpha males into becoming whining liberal cuckflakes by 2020.

From the helicopter news feed in DC it's looking pretty sparse down there. There's no way he's going to match Obama's crowds. I hope we've got some sort of spin on that ready to go? Don't blatantly lie, though. I don't want to hear about how the empty areas are actually *full* of people but regrettably everyone is dressed in the same neutral colours as the empty areas thereby creating the *illusion* that no one is there, or whatever.

Good luck. Looking forward to America being great again tomorrow.

Best,

M.

From: M [mailto: m@axworthy.com]
To: Sean Spicer [mailto: seanspicer78534@whitehouse.gov]
Sent: 23rd January 2017 23:05
Subject: WT actual F

Sean,

I've seen some bad days in the office in my time but watching you yesterday was like witnessing the whole office being sucked into a black hole.

This was Day One.

Day. One.

Within minutes of approaching the podium, tensely gripping the sides like a drunk at a toilet bowl, you had alienated every journalist in the room by accusing them of falsely reporting the inauguration attendance.

These are White House reporters, baggy-pants. No, they're not meant to be your friends, but it *is* your responsibility to establish a symbiotic relationship with them so they write their pieces in an objective frame of mind. Within forty minutes of your first press conference, your frenzied sulk has ensured that will never happen. And what's particularly mind-boggling about your potty performance is that you clearly don't believe the thing you're throwing a tantrum over: you were simply acting as a conduit for your boss in the hope of a pat on the head and a tickle under the chin.

Normally I don't mind a bit of falsehood at the podium if it's to get the right message across, but this was a wholly unnecessary spat about crowd numbers to massage the new president's extremely fragile ego. That's what you are: a 24-hour ego masseuse, not a press secretary.

I know the next four years are going to be tough for you: the President is not going to stop tweeting half-formed thoughts in shouty caps-lock at two in the morning, and he sure as shit isn't going to run them past a jellyfish in a pinstripe suit before pressing send. But barking at the press that a picture of 10 people is actually a picture of 10,000, or whatever you claimed, then refusing to take any questions and stomping off is bad form. It's really bad form, Sean. Everyone has lost their respect for you. OK, admittedly no one knew who you were 24 hours ago, but in the small gap between finding out who you were and your mouth opening, they had respect for you, trust me.

If you're to carry on in this position, my advice would be to use your own judgement from time to time. Unchain yourself from the massage table and be a human up there.

Oh, and get a suit that fits. You looked like you were being eaten by your shirt collar.

Best,

M.

NOTES

How TM needs to come across when she visits Trump at the White House tomorrow - Operation 'To Be and NOT to Be':

- To be eager to secure a new special relationship with the US.

  NOT to be desperate to do any deal with Trump ahead of being rinsed, kicked up the arse and whipped with a wet towel by the EU.

- To be relaxed in the company of the President.

  NOT to look like she's trapped in a sex museum.

- To be happy to butter him up with compliments on his election victory.

  NOT to shiver involuntarily with repulsion afterwards, like she does when she has to walk around a factory.

- To be forthright about the fact that they
  disagree on some issues.

  NOT ever to mention these issues. Ever. Not
  even in her sleep.

- To be prepared to have difficult negotiations
  with Trump over trade.

  NOT to acknowledge that any negotiations with
  Trump are pointless because a) he will always
  have the upper hand in trade talks with a UK
  weakened by Brexit, and b) he doesn't know how
  to negotiate or bargain, he just sits with his
  arms folded, waiting for you to agree with him,
  like a toddler does.

How Trump needs to come across when TM visits
tomorrow - Operation: 'Be Normal, Please God Be
Normal'

- To appear supportive on the UK's Brexit
  situation.

NOT to come across like a vulture in a Tex Avery cartoon, shaking salt on Britain's bloated carcass, licking his wet lips and shoving his napkin into his collar.

- To reiterate that Brexit was the best outcome for the British people.

  NOT to reveal at any point that his knowledge of Europe is limited to 'Euro Truck Simulator 2'.

- To be warm and friendly during any moment of physical contact (hugging, kissing the cheek, shaking hands, etc.)

  NOT to be as awkward as me when I tried online dating circa 2003.

- To be alert and interested at all times.

  NOT to look at his watch, scratch the back of his head and look around the room as if all he wants to do is watch 'Ice Age 4' in bed with a bucket of chicken.

Can you believe it?? After all that planning and preparation to ensure a smooth, gaffe-free visit by the Prime Minister, and President Pumpkin-Chops goes and tells the world a mere five days later that Muslims are banned from travelling to the US.

There's a lot of pressure on TM to cancel _her_ state visit to Washington later this year but I don't see how they can. Great Britain literally has no overseas allies now apart from bits of Canada, Tanzania and that place in Spain that has the 'Only Fools and Horses' pub.

Oh. Dear. God. How much longer can this nightmare continue? When will I get my allotment?

AXWORTHY GLOBAL

PO BOX 998 · ALDINGTON ST · KW17 5EH

From: M

To: Λ

Date: 13/02/17

Heading: New Downing Street Adviser – potential recruit?

Message:

Dear A,

I hope this letter finds you well. Although if it finds you at all that would be a good start.

It feels like we're in the eye of the storm at the moment, what with Trump turning the White House into an Orwellian soft-play centre and Theresa May losing the plot over Brexit and going – to borrow the parlance of my 17-year-old nephew – totes batshit cray.

I had hoped with time on our side we might be able to put things right, but it seems from the surveillance at Downing Street that time is precisely what we don't have any more. From what I gather, the PM's closest advisers are looking to hire a chief adviser who, according to one aide, 'should reflect the ever-growing demand for a more resolute move to the right'. Or in other words, an anti-liberal, anti-antifa 'Pocket Trump' to steer May away from the centre-right and capitalise on this appetite in the west for . . . well, social prejudice and bigotry? Seems weird that a lot of human beings want that back. I can understand people getting nostalgic for SodaStreams or *The A-Team* or chunky sneakers, but fascism? I really don't understand. It wasn't great the first time round. I'll have to leave that to the anthropologists to figure out in fifty years' time.

My sources suggest the leading candidate for the PM's chief adviser job is Chris Catcher, a popular blogger and vlogger who has written hundreds of articles on his own personal website about the disenfranchised white man. He has achieved notoriety online for his militant right-wing views, which have earned him half a million followers on Twitter and a blue tick to boot. With this guy at the top of the tree, Axworthy's control is severely jeopardised. Someone like him will never listen to us.

However, I did some digging and it turns out Catcher tried to put a men's rights activist movement together in 2012, which failed spectacularly. He binned the whole site after it had imploded but thanks to our friends over in IT, I've managed to get some screenshots of a number of webpages. I think there's enough there to ensure his chunky sneakers never set foot inside No. 10.

Let me know what you think.

Best,

M.

About Us

The United Men's Movement (or 'UMM') was founded in 2010 by celebrated men's rights campaigner Chris Oatcher (not pictured, that's just a stock photograph of a businessman with a megaphone).

Chris first discovered he was a talented forward thinker when he was prevented from entering a nightclub in 1998. While he watched a line of women with short skirts and low-cut tops enter the club to dance the night away provocatively, Chris remained out in the cold, figuratively and literally because it was November and he was only wearing a light jacket.

The reason why he was wearing a light jacket in November is because if he wore his thick winter coat, he'd have to spend half an hour in the queue for the cloakroom. And it's a major hassle collecting it at the end of the night too, particularly if you're pissed out of your pot. Sorry. This is supposed to be the 'About Us' page. I've gone off the subject a bit here. I'll start a new paragraph.

Chris Catcher:
LEADER

Chris Catcher (born January 20th 1977) is a British men's rights campaigner, activist, author, educator, blogger and vlogger. He is the founding member of the most prominent men's rights movement in the UK today – the United Men's Movement (or 'UMM').

He has written three self-published books on men's rights, gender politics and how women are culpable for blame culture.

CHRIS CATCHER

MEN ARE REALISTS, WOMEN ARE AERIALISTS

From the bestselling author of 'FEMINEXISM - The Hyprocrisy of the Modern Feminist'

Despite having numerous girlfriends, he felt disconnected from them and rather than find a job, he began researching what he believed to be a growing cultural breakdown between genders. His parents were delighted.

The research culminated in his first book *Men are Realists, Women are Aerialists* in which he stated men were the grounded and sensible half of all heterosexual couples, whereas women were the idealistic half, forever raising their relationship goals to unrealistic levels and subsequently blaming their male partners for when these ambitions were not realised.

'Men are forever having to prove their worth to their girlfriends and wives. Women should realise that they will never find a flawless man. When it comes to dating, women need to lower their expectations right from the off. The moment a woman greets a man for the first time on a date, she shouldn't assume him to be an unblemished vision of modern masculinity like the Duke of Cambridge or Steve Redgrave, she needs to address immediately the method by which he will disappoint her and – most importantly – love him for it.'

Men are Realists, Women are Aerialists, Chris Catcher 2000

Chris founded the United Men's Movement after watching a line of women walk into a nightclub ahead of him. Their gender somehow granted them access to a premier Barking nightspot which directly or indirectly resulted in refused entry for Chris. It was at that moment that he decided to turn his years of essays and research into a movement; to take his message out onto the street – or in this case, an online forum for disenfranchised men that began life as a website for *Fast and Furious* fan art.

Today the United Men's Movement grows exponentially, putting men's issues firmly in the spotlight and reducing the damage committed by the secret feminist agenda in this country.

Please send your messages of thanks via the **Contact** box.

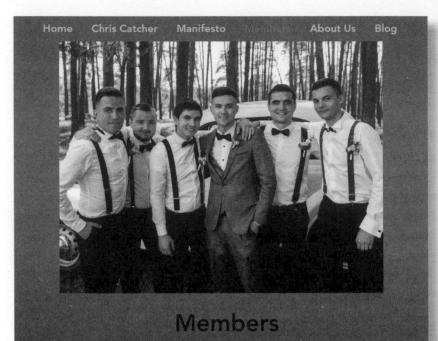

Members

Adam Beckett. 23. Deputy Leader. Adam joined the movement only a month ago but has already shown his courage, capacity and endeavour to provide transport to and from the town hall. Chris met Adam through a shared employer. Adam was a little wet behind the ears when he first joined the movement, not fully attuned to the damaging prejudices this country has been witnessing at the hands of hysterical and dogmatic women for decades. But Chris took him under his wing and opened his eyes to the injustices of being a white male man in 2017. Adam was thankful.

Tim Whitelock. 50. Tim is a passionate member of UMM and a wealthy businessman with a heated indoor swimming pool. Tim first came aboard when his own men's rights movement, the International Men's Movement or IMM, was forced to disband after repeated failures to recruit a single member. Tim was happy to step aside and have his movement absorbed into Chris's.

Sharon Catcher. 55. Sharon is a woman but despite this, her spirit is tremendous. A close relation of Chris, Sharon is the appointed administrator for the movement, providing the minutes for meetings, organising travel, making packed lunches and running the movement's headquarters from her semi-detached house in Epping where Chris is temporarily residing. He will be moving out soon.

Sydney Pepper. 25. Sydney was our first FAF (Female Against Feminism) because it's not just men who wish to knock women off their self-aggrandising pedestal. Over the last few years Sydney has realised that her dreams of becoming a model or actress or singer or TV presenter or TV house expert are being curtailed by an unjust media agenda – fuelled by harmful feminists – that promotes intelligence over beauty.

Sydney first joined UMM when she was bumped from a shortlist of hopefuls for a forthcoming gardening programme on UK Mulch (Sky Channel 723), losing out to a woman who although boasting a Kew Diploma in Horticulture, had terrible fashion sense and fat legs.

Manifesto

We will be publishing the full manifesto here just as soon as we can ascertain how to make the PDF work. Meanwhile here are some sample objectives taken from the official document.

Overview

It has become increasingly obvious to the United Men's Movement that even though men earn and contribute more to the economy, the political systems in operation in this country have been designed to benefit women only.

As a result, we have seen a social and cultural shift/shifts towards female absolutism instigated by the unstoppable locomotive of destruction that is modern feminism. UMM aims to bring a halt to this/these dangerous shift/shifts and reinstate the equilibrium that favours male levelheadedness over female hysteria.

Employment

There is no such thing as a glass ceiling, except for literal glass ceilings. The simple fact is women don't work as hard as men and expect areas of their job to be undertaken by other people on their behalf.

The reason for this expectation is because for centuries women in employment have devoted vast sections of their working day to self-care such as applying makeup, adjusting hairstyles and changing footwear, and when it became apparent they were only doing half their duties, assistants were recruited and favours pulled. And yet despite this unwavering obsession with their looks, when a man tells a woman she has a nice face or a well-rounded bosom, his flattering comment is thrown back in his face.

Women's brains are not designed for science, maths, engineering, technology and medicine and should therefore be discouraged from applying in these fields unless they want to be humiliated by their mental insufficiency further down the line.

UMM propose new laws that limit opportunities for women in certain areas of employment, narrowing their choices and therefore giving them a greater chance of success.

Political Systems

Why is the Commission for Gender Equality so pro-female? Don't men deserve equality too? No. That's because the commission is a facade, a smokescreen for a vehemently anti-male agenda that will soon influence other commissions, initiatives and policies where the role of men will be reduced significantly.

You may ask yourself why women would go out of their way to crush the rights of men when all they should want is the balance redressed. Sure, on the face of it, it makes no sense at all why they would act like this and you might even conclude that the motivation behind the United Men's Movement is due to something far more deep-rooted and psychological such as a lack of parental affection. But you'd be wrong.

The fact is women are motivated by revenge. Pure and simple.

UMM would introduce a new a system of policy-making whereby women are allowed to make policies once they have been vetted by a government-appointed group of men. This group would be called the Male Scrutiny Commission.

Justice in the UK (or Lack Thereof)

Feminists and feminist thinking have inveigled their way into the criminal justice system in this country, putting pressure on anyone who may favour a man over a woman in a court of law.

The fact is, the long-established prejudices of the divorce courts that portray all fathers as a cross between Jake LaMotta and a pissed wolf have spilled over into other areas of law, so if you're a woman and you've been accused of a crime, whether it be becoming a terrorist or stealing an apple, make sure there's a bystander with the male chromosome in your sights to pin it on.

UMM would overhaul the justice system from scratch to create a more reasoned, sensible and conciliatory approach to law regardless of gender.

We would also bring back firing squads.

Do check back here to see if we've sorted out the PDF.

Private letter to President Trump suggests the existence of a covert organisation within the White House – 28 March 2017

WebiLeaks has come into ownership of a secret letter sent by the President of the United States' press secretary Sean Spicer to Donald Trump himself.

The letter is one of confusion and anxiety and refers to people working for a secret organisation to whom Sean Spicer is seemingly answerable. Raging paranoia on Spicer's part, or is there truth to the whispers that have been plaguing the US AND UK governments of an affiliation with a shadowy institution pulling the strings? What follows is a direct quote from Spicer's leaked letter:

'It is becoming increasingly difficult to do my job due to the level of interference I have to put up with from the other team. Take last week as an example. As you instructed, I relayed your tweets to the press that you had been the subject of surveillance from British intelligence.' [Mr Spicer here referring to a *Fox News* report which so far has produced no evidence of spying by the British Government but which the President felt compelled to tweet about anyway.]

'I thought I was doing a swell job until M calls me in the office after the press conference and barks a string of insults down the line, most of which are incomprehensible because of his English cockney accent. Why must he do this? Why must I listen to him? Shouldn't I only listen to you? Why am I getting these mixed messages?'

Mr Spicer goes on to make a bold suggestion.

'I am aware this organisation has been advising presidents for like half a century – M himself has been around since the Lewinsky scandal, I understand – but if they are clearly at odds with you and your policies, why employ them? It's only serving to make my job more difficult. And let me tell you something, my job is difficult enough! Like, full-time, bam-bam-bam, know what I mean? Sometimes I even have to work on a Saturday, which has really had an impact on "Seany's Family Fun Time".'

At this point Mr Spicer goes into minute detail about what 'Seany's Family Fun Time' is and what it entails. We have taken the decision to omit this section.

It is unclear which organisation Spicer is referring to, and who 'M' is. It is also unclear whether the President even received this letter and consequently acted upon it.

If you have any information relating to the issues in the letter, please get in touch. We treat all emails with the strictest confidence. Except for the emails we leak, obviously. We just mean the emails to us.

Nikki – Arrange a meeting with heads of depts and try and get A in on the call too. We need to do something about Sean Spicer.

29 March 2017 17.03

Hey Curtis, hope you don't mind my DMing you, just wondered if you wanted to chat to the Messenger about the triggering of Article 50 today?

Lewis Potterhouse @RealLewisPotterhouse

Hi Lewis, this is a surprise. Why do you want to chat to me? I'm just a nobody blogger with 320 followers!

Curtis Poll @CurtisInside

I can tell from your tweets and blog posts that you must have some sort of insider information. No one can know what you know and not be at the heart of Westminster. I thought getting a few comments from you might beef up the piece I have to write.

Lewis Potterhouse @RealLewisPotterhouse

Trust me, I know nothing. I merely speculate how the machine works. I don't operate it.

Curtis Poll @CurtisInsider

Nice try. You want to keep your identity a secret. I get that. You can remain anonymous. I would just like to get your expert opinion on record.

Lewis Potterhouse @RealLewisPotterhouse

I am far from being an expert. I'm just an armchair pundit.

Curtis Poll @CurtisInside

Well, for an armchair pundit you sure know a lot about the myriad cross-pollinating shitstorms currently occurring at Westminster.

Lewis Potterhouse @RealLewisPotterhouse

Lucky guesses, I guess.

Curtis Poll @CurtisInside

Come on, pal. Don't be so mealy-mouthed. I'm struggling to get any source to tell me the truth today. I need some of your explosive intel to get this on the front page.

Lewis Potterhouse @RealLewisPotterhouse

First of all, don't call me pal, I'm not an antenna connector. And second of all, you write for the Daily Messenger: your readers don't want to know the truth, they want immigrant scare stories alongside a picture of Kate Middleton looking forlorn.

Curtis Poll @CurtisInside

You sound irritable. Having a bad day at the office?

Lewis Potterhouse @RealLewisPotterhouse

Stop digging. I do not work in Downing St, OK? I don't have anything to do with the current government. Believe me, if I was responsible for this gaggle of narrow-minded bunions, I'd have grown my beard out like Michael Sheen and opened a nautical gift shop on the Isle of Mull by now.

Curtis Poll @CurtisInside

Do you agree with Michael Heseltine that this is 'the worst peacetime decision taken by any modern postwar government'?

Lewis Potterhouse @RealLewisPotterhouse

Of course I do, because I have a brain that isn't just a big ball of Union Jack bunting.

Curtis Poll @CurtisInside

Can I quote you on that?

Lewis Potterhouse @RealLewisPotterhouse

No.

Curtis Poll @CurtisInside

Can I ask if you know anything about this secret organisation that was alluded to by the White House press secretary a few weeks ago?

Lewis Potterhouse @RealLewisPotterhouse

Muting in 5 . . . 4 . . . 3 . . .

Curtis Poll @CurtisInside

I'm giving you a national platform to air your views.

Lewis Potterhouse @RealLewisPotterhouse

The national platform being the Daily Messenger, whose sole aim is to turn quiet Middle Englanders into permanently outraged xenophobic dogmatists. I can't tell you how many uncles, aunts, neighbours and school friends I've excommunicated because of you. I'd rather air my views from inside a chemical toilet at a flooded metal festival. I'll pass.

. . . 2 . . . 1.

Curtis Poll @CurtisInside

I'm in Saudi Arabia, where PM May is trying to sell arms. Normal working week, really. It was a toss-up between this or escorting Liam Fox to the Philippines as he tries to forge stronger bonds with President Duterte, who has killed 7,000 of his own people for drugs offences. Other cabinet members are on similar missions to find billions of pounds' worth of trade with non-EU countries this week. Quite why we're opting for leaders with obscene human rights violations is unclear. I hear Australia are keen to do business with us. New Zealand? No, no, let's put Liam Fox on a plane to the Philippines for him to stand awkwardly like a soggy cake next to a man who encourages his citizens to murder drug addicts without trial. Nothing morally compromising about that.

I would say this is a low point for Liam Fox but when has there ever been a high point? The man has forged a career out of never venturing too far from base camp.

NOTES

19th April 2017

General Election Thoughts

Some thoughts on May's announcement for a snap general election on June 8.

Do not under any circumstances arrange for the public to meet the PM face-to-face. Crowds are fine but no 'one-on-ones'. The public at the moment is an unpredictable swarm and the thought of Doris from Denshaw cornering Mrs May in a chip shop and demanding a blue passport by Christmas sends shivers down my spine.

She CAN'T take any risks.

Actually when I said crowds are fine, I've decided crowds are not fine either. Crowds make her uncomfortable too. Maybe I should put together a list?

List of locations that are acceptable for the PM to meet voters during this election:

- A haunted theme park
- An abandoned cooling tower
- The sunken remains of a warship
- A rural bus stop on a Sunday
- A derelict castle
- A hovercraft
- Any non-operational submarine base
- Any cinema during a screening of 'King Arthur: Legend of the Sword'
- A neglected chemical factory
- A field with no footpath access

9th June 2017

'Spectacularly backfired'

Those are the two buzzwords this morning. Everyone's using them. No other words sum up the result of Theresa May's gamble on an early election. Let's face it, no other words would work. I bet even her husband Philip said, 'Well, that spectacularly backfired, didn't it, dear?' while pouring the tea at breakfast this morning.

So, what went wrong? Why did May's campaign and manifesto fail to convince British voters at the ballot box?

Because she put the slogan 'Strong and Stable' at the heart of her campaign. And inevitably she would be pictured standing next to that slogan at a factory or on a podium in a shopping centre. And those two things, side by side, never looked right. She never looked strong and she never looked stable. A more fitting slogan would have been 'Clueless and Uncomfortable'.

You could also put the blame on Mrs May's chief strategists, Nick Timothy and Fiona Hill, the architects of the manifesto, who made enemies of cabinet ministers by leaving them out of the big campaign decisions. I say 'architects', but that's a bit of a contradiction, as what they ended up doing was tearing down the house someone else had built and then setting fire to the rubble.

Where does this leave the PM?

Well, she has two clear options: one is to do a deal with the Democratic Unionist Party, which would mean forking over a lot of cash from the 'magic money tree' that Mrs May categorically said did not exist, but which I can confirm, categorically, bloody well does. And the second option is to resign and let Boris Johnson succeed her, because let's face it, we all know that's where this is going. It's going to happen. One day we are going to be ruled over by that blithering thatched beehive of catastrophe and we're all going to suffer greatly from it. Except very wealthy Conservative donors, of course. The ring of steel around them will be even stronger once Johnson takes to the throne.

So on the face of it, option one is preferable. And that's going to cause unbearable carnage too.

What a wonderful few years we have ahead. More tea?

CP

21 June 2017

Warren Marks Publishing
4 Tonbridge Street
London
W8 9LT

Dear Hannah,

Please excuse the rather archaic method of communication, but as you have probably surmised, it's pretty much the only avenue open to me if we are to make this work. As a trusted friend, I have no doubt that once you read this letter you will shred it, burn the shreds and then use the ashes of the shreds as some sort of snail deterrent in your lovely garden.

It's been a nearly a year now since Axworthy assigned me the task of improving the 'policies, image and status' of Theresa May and, to be honest, I'm surprised I'm still in a job. I guess they know it's virtually an unachievable goal and so they let me toil away in the hope I might score the odd point here and there. But ultimately, she remains a universally derided, glum-looking, aimless, clueless, mechanical chicken. Whatever hope there was for her as PM, it's fading faster than Donald Trump's tan in a sauna.

The last eleven months have exceeded any nightmare I could have envisaged. And therefore I've decided I've got to get out. Now. I want to shift gear and embrace what I thought might be my next career move in twenty years' time: that of amateur historian.

When I turn on the television and watch Michael Portillo fart-arsing about on steam engines with his privileged sausage-grin, clad in items of incandescent clothing that don't so much clash as torture one another, I feel quite the pang of jealousy. And so I see this as my first step towards superseding him and his monstrously dull ilk.

It is without a doubt that Theresa May is the worst prime minister we've ever had, and what my book hopes to achieve is to present this statement as cast-iron fact by comparing her to all other British prime ministers. Well, not all of them. I mean, who gives two figs about the seventeenth-century lot and their 3rd Viscounts of Twitherington-Upon-Fluffshires.

Please find enclosed six samples for my anonymous book (working title *Just How Awful Is Theresa May?*).

Hope you enjoy it. I didn't.

Best,

M.

Just How Awful Is Theresa May?

EXAMPLE ONE: DAVID CAMERON

Ultimately, David Cameron is responsible for the barn of manure we currently find ourselves locked inside in the year 2017. However, he did win the 2015 general election pretty convincingly, and oversaw a lot of important events such as the withdrawal of British troops from two catastrophic wars and the legalisation of same-sex marriage.

So there are a few chinks of sunlight in front of which David Cameron can bring up a comfortable chair and position himself. This will at least help him forget momentarily that he made the fatal error of including the EU Referendum pledge in his 2015 manifesto just to win back a few jingoistic, jam-for-brain idiots from UKIP.

Theresa May, on the other hand, is so ineffectual as a prime minister that she can't even do a deal with the DUP, a party of weasel-faced hypocrites, despite being a weasel-faced hypocrite herself. That's just how staggeringly awful she is.

So yes, David Cameron – an undeniably thunderous boil, but as a prime minister? Simply not as awful as Theresa May.

EXAMPLE TWO: MARGARET THATCHER

Now you'd think that, given the prolonged periods of high unemployment, social unrest, rioting, unnecessary wars and capitalist greed, Margaret Thatcher would be towering over Theresa May in terms of prime ministerial awfulness, but I suggest that this is not the case for one simple reason.

Margaret Thatcher had legions of passionate supporters for well over a decade: men and women who believed in her cause; who would fight for it; who believed in her values, her ideals, her vision of Britain – even though that vision would make a normal, compassionate human being vomit for ever.

Theresa May, on the other hand, never has, and will never, enjoy such passionate support. In fact, she's managed to repel everyone in the country, left, right *and* centre, within a fortnight: an unprecedented situation for the Prime Minister of Great Britain and Northern Ireland to be in. We're essentially being led by a can of pepper spray.

Margaret Thatcher was the face of hatred and division for ten years, but she was simply not as awful as Theresa May, who is currently governing the country with the assuredness and stability of a dizzy bear with fireworks for paws.

EXAMPLE THREE: ANTHONY EDEN

Now, like Thatcher, Anthony Eden *was* awful. An absolute cottage pie of a prime minister, who instigated the monumental blunder of deploying military force against Egypt over the Suez Canal. When it became apparent that he would not receive the backing of his allies, Eden had to withdraw his troops and resign, cementing his legacy as nothing more than a picnic hamper of horses' arses.

However, prior to becoming prime minister, Anthony Eden was a comparatively principled and courageous man, who resigned as Foreign Secretary in 1938 in protest at then prime minister Neville Chamberlain's policy of appeasing fascist dictators Hitler and Mussolini.

On 16th August 2017, Theresa May refused to cancel President Trump's planned state visit to the UK, after he appeared to sympathise with white supremacists in Charlottesville, preferring instead to express her outrage that, due to essential maintenance, the general public wouldn't be able to hear Big Ben's chimes for a while.

Big Ben's chimes.

EXAMPLE FOUR: HAROLD MACMILLAN

Harold Macmillan was a fiercely determined prime minister who, after telling the British people that they'd never had it so good, promptly ensured that they never had 'it' ever again by freezing wages to stop rising inflation, thereby pricking a balloon full of shit right in front of his own face and signalling his inevitable demise.

However, despite a permanent facial expression that suggested he'd rather be at home eating a pie, Harold Macmillan was a ruthless and calculating little moustachioed grass snake. And no event illustrated this more than his decision to sack a third of his cabinet in one evening to lose all the stockpiled deadwood, which even by today's standards is a breathtakingly Machiavellian dick move.

Theresa May could only dream of such self-confidence. As it is, she's a prisoner within her own cabinet, shackled to the pillowcase of asbestos otherwise known as Boris Johnson, the worst Foreign Secretary in living memory. Johnson is a man who thinks he can just dismiss the national disgust towards him as a bit of a lark, like he was a sitcom character or a pantomime villain, when in actual face he's a dangerously inept, odious, arrogant, chauvinistic blobfish.

Harold Macmillan may have his critics for what he did to the economy in the sixties but at least we know that, had he momentarily lost control of his faculties and appointed a poisonous sack of sausage meat as Foreign Secretary, he would almost certainly have flung that appointment under a bus the moment it made him look bad. And that is why he is not as awful as Theresa May.

EXAMPLE FIVE: JAMES CALLAGHAN

James Callaghan was a tornado of bad decisions in a suit. Not only did he preside over the infamous Winter of Discontent, but he also implemented – as Home Secretary – the Commonwealth Immigrants Act of 1968, which effectively blocked many Kenyan Asians from entering the UK after Kenya introduced its ruthless 'Africanisation' policy.

But in the same year Callaghan passed the Race Relations Act, making it illegal to refuse employment, housing or education on the basis of ethnic background. At least as Home Secretary he didn't have a strategy to create hostility and division, unlike Theresa May with her mistreatment of the Windrush Generation and her 'Go Home or Face Arrest' vans – which sounds like the sort of idea a UKIP supporter would scribble down on a fat sketch pad with a big souvenir-shop pencil.

Now, thanks to the dismissal of Amber Rudd, who inadvertently misled the Home Affairs Select Committee on the issue of illegal immigration and, on a broader note, displayed all the ministerial qualities of a drunken sea lion walking into a hat stand, we're beginning to see the true extent of Theresa May's dogmatic and cold-hearted intentions.

We're being governed by a morally bankrupt, surreptitious bully who somehow thinks that standing with her feet unnaturally far apart like she's about to lay an egg will make us forget that she's the worst prime minister we've ever had. Seriously. She's awful. She's awful and she needs to go.

EXAMPLE SIX: JOHN MAJOR

Despite a record-breaking election victory in 1992, which turned Neil Kinnock into a gibbering, inconsequential sandwich, John Major was not blessed with a honeymoon period.

In September of the same year, the UK was forced to withdraw the pound sterling from the Exchange Rate Mechanism, on a day that would soon become known as 'A Bunch of Catastrophic Arseholes Flush Three Billion Pounds Down the Toilet' Day. Virtually overnight, John Major went from the 'mastermind of the '92 election' to a universally derided, financially incompetent melon.

However, despite being the face of a decaying party populated by blaggers, daggers and illicit shaggers, John Major did work tirelessly towards lasting peace in Northern Ireland, paving the way for the Good Friday Agreement and establishing for him a more favourable legacy than he might have otherwise received.

Theresa May's legacy will *not* be favourable. Theresa May's legacy will be that of a perished ham, packed with explosives, bursting in front of our eyes for ever, thanks to her Brexit deal which would – among other things – ensure a *new* period of uncertainty on both sides of the Irish border.

Although let's not forget the fact that she's also persevering with delivering on a referendum result that's drowning in allegations of illegal funding, Russian-backed social media manipulation and far-right shit-stirring.

And rather than address the obvious slide into filthy far-right politics that the Leave campaign had been planning all along, she has instead come up with a Brexit deal that has somehow been opposed by everyone, further bolstering her position as the most incompetent, desperate and embarrassing prime minister we've ever had and who makes John Major look like bleeding Thor.

And because everyone thinks her Brexit solution is just a vase of potty thought-burps, we're now marching hopelessly towards a No Deal Brexit Britain, with Theresa May at the helm, which is like putting a wasp in charge of a wedding.

In a normal, sane world, Theresa May would *not* be leading us into this sort of terrifying hellscape. She wouldn't even be left in charge of separating paper from plastic on recycling day. But here we are.

Still.

4 Tonbridge St
Holland Hill
London
W8 9LT

3 July 2017

Axworthy Global
PO Box 998
Aldington Street
KW17 5EH

Dear M,

Many thanks for your letter and your examples.

Although it would give me great satisfaction to be responsible for your transition from adviser to historian, I do feel that an entire book dedicated to insulting Theresa May is a little niche.

If, for instance, you could widen your scope, allowing you to provide a fresh and interesting critique on a number of British politicians, then we might be able to have a chat. As it is, this just feels like a rant: a calculated, methodical and well-structured rant, but a rant nonetheless.

Sorry not to be more positive on this occasion but my door is always open.

And, as ever, if you want to write that exposé about your organisation, just let me know.

Yours,

Hannah

Dear All,

In light of a spate of public apologies recently, please find below an Apology Template that I've been working on. This is a catch-all apology for a range of indiscretions, which should hopefully save time in the long run. Normally with an MP apology story I would opt for prolonged moments of remorse with plenty of room for redemption and sincerity, but unfortunately the speed at which the current government is imploding means we haven't got time to stop and have a custard cream, let alone fashion a protracted tabloid confession story.

Therefore, I have produced the following template to speed up the narrative and put to bed any and all matters in need of a serious walking back. Please keep a copy and adapt as you need.

Dear [Whoever]

I would like to take full responsibility for the mistakes I have made.

I apologise to my constituents and to Parliament. I recognise now that my attempts to [whatever positive spin you can put on the criminally underthought action they actually took] were in conflict with my duty as an MP.

Despite this being an apology (which it absolutely is, and a sincere one at that), I would like to make it clear that my attempts to cover up the truth were only so I could protect [yes, we all know this should now read 'my own', but please substitute my constituents' / the country's] interests. If I felt that being honest was a viable option, I would have absolutely taken it. Regrettably this was not the case.

The last [period of time] has been difficult for me and I'm grateful to my family, friends and colleagues for standing by me and letting me know that their view of me has not changed, because ultimately what I did wasn't really that bad in the scheme of things. Although I am sorry for it and this is still an apology.

The reputation of the House has taken a severe blow in recent years and it troubles me to think that I have in some way contributed to this. Of course, my contribution was small in relation to other MPs' indiscretions – minuscule in fact, really, really tiny, some would say hardly worth mentioning let alone apologising for (not me, though, I am apologising now and this is still an apology) – nevertheless I feel I am duty bound to make amends for my poor judgement and I apologise. I am sorry.

I fully accept that my actions caused some distress (though not a great deal) to those I unavoidably deceived and I would like to make it clear that I will be sitting down with them in the coming weeks to fully explain my actions in the hope that they, too, will understand, much like my family, friends and colleagues did. Which they did. Quite easily and without any prompting.

I will also be offering to make a donation to a charity of their choosing as a signal of my intentions to mend any division. The donation will not be modest. This is because I feel the contribution should match the scale of the indiscretion.

For which, once again, I apologise.

Yours sincerely,

[MP's name]

Diary: Sunday 20th May 2018

It's been a tough 2018 so far, for so many reasons, but I did enjoy the Royal Wedding of Hazza and Meghan yesterday. For one specific reason.

The wedding was covered by an independent production company by the name of Jubilant Corgi Productions. Their chief aim was to cover the occasion and make a fast buck by turning them into souvenir DVDs.

Through various contacts they approached me to provide advice and consultation for their royal commentator, who they feared wasn't quite prepared due to some issues in his private life. They didn't know about Axworthy but they knew about me. Somehow people are finding out about me. This is a little disconcerting. Anyway, after a brief meeting I decided I didn't want to pursue the position. Maybe one day I'll go freelance but not today. The job was going to cause more trouble than it was worth, and anyway, how hard is it to describe nicely dressed people waving for six hours?

Out of curiosity I bought the DVD today in WH Smith's, taped to some dreadful souvenir magazine. From what I could gather, it seems they did not find a replacement for me. The royal commentator was unrehearsed, inadvertently offensive and staggeringly inept throughout. It made great viewing.

Here are some of the highlights:

'The spectators on the grounds of Windsor Castle have been specially selected to be here, away from the larger, more "eccentric" spectators outside. This is to – um, well, I mean this in the nicest possible way – to sort the wheat from the chaff. The royal couple certainly do not want to see . . . I don't know, a dubious-looking man in a Union Jack suit clutching a dozen terrifying dolls. Not on their special day anyway.

'St George's Chapel is absolutely vibrant with the

scent of the flowers here. It's absolutely intoxicating, it reminds me a lot of the Glade PlugIn that I've got in my downstairs toilet. Wild Rose Blossom, or something like that. It came in very handy last week, actually, because I had a delivery from Yodel and the driver asked if he could use my toilet and I swear to God he was in there for about thirty-five minutes. It was mortifying, primarily because I don't permit anyone to use the downstairs toilet for um . . . "not number ones".

'Harry looking nervous now. This is when William needs to reassure his little brother that everything is going to work out, that everything is going to be OK. Not in life. I just mean in the next few hours. I'm talking about the ceremony, not the marriage. No one knows if the marriage is going to work out.

'Prince Harry and Prince William arrive at Windsor Castle looking extremely well groomed in their black military coats and pristine cotton gloves. I'm a great advocate of cotton gloves, actually. Every night I apply E45 hand cream and whack on a pair of crisp white ones before I go to bed. I have anxiety-related eczema as a result of my divorce.

'I hope Prince Harry doesn't wake up one morning on the cusp of <u>his</u> forty-second birthday, staring at his white cotton gloves, alone in bed, trying to fathom out how love became such a cold, icy dagger to the heart. But Meghan seems really nice, so it's unlikely that'll happen.'

13th June 2018

Briefing for White House Comms. Team

Trump and Kim – top tips on how to avoid war today

Promote any general politeness/courtesy (shaking hands, smiling, etc.) as being symbolic of a strong bond between the two nations and the two leaders – even though they've only met for the first time today and all previous communication has been a succession of name-calling tweets that read like they were written by 6-year-olds with a fondness for undiluted squash.

Try to find common ground, e.g. both Kim and Trump have had to take important business decisions to maintain their status – Donald Trump branched out from real estate and attached his name to numerous products and services ranging from energy drinks to beefsteaks, and Kim Jong-un murdered a bunch of people. Peas in a pod, really.

Keyword here. bromance. We must make it seem as if by the end of the day the two leaders would be happy to be in charge of each other's stag parties. Although I imagine any stag party run by these two would inevitably involve more carnage than the *Saw* franchise.

Can we have any banter about Kim's hair? I mean, that is a sharp cut. Who's his hairdresser? The nerves of steel that person must possess getting the blending right with the clippers. Hats off.

The signing of the denuclearisation statement is the showpiece of the day. I know it's ostensibly two men writing their names with fancy pens, but it's got to look more glitzy than the Oscars and be more entertaining than *Hamilton*. Plus, we must ensure we don't give Trump that pen with the ship floating in it. He was so side-tracked by it last time that it took him forty minutes to remember what it was he was signing.

Is there anything we can do about taking the praise Trump reserves for himself and giving some of it to Kim? We know POTUS improvises at least five paragraphs of unremitting admiration for his own abilities during these events so I think it would be a nice gesture if he let Kim deliver some of these fawning passages of self-congratulatory wank, rather than himself (?). Worth suggesting.

Also is there any way we can nudge Kim into firmer territory when it comes to disarmament? I don't like the phrase 'working towards the denuclearisation of the Korean peninsula'. We can all *work towards* something, but it doesn't mean it's going to happen. I can *work towards* a six-pack and pectoral muscles like cereal bowls, but it doesn't mean I'm going to start going to the gym or stop eating salted caramel fudge.

Diary: Tuesday 10th July 2018

Wonderful news about the successful rescue of the boys trapped in a cave in Thailand yesterday. It got me thinking. If the UK government were in charge of that rescue operation, they'd have added more boys.

Prime Minister May: Hello. Before you start—

M: Three.

Prime Minister May: Yes, but listen—

M: Three parliamentary defeats in a single day for your EU deal.

Prime Minister May: I am aware of this.

M: Back in October, there were many political commentators who had numerous opinions as to what you should have said or done during your conference speech. Do you know what I wished you had done? I wished you had come onto the stage, doing that dance that you do, and I wished you had danced right past the podium. I wished you had danced across the stage and exited out the other side straight into a waiting horsebox, which would then have been nailed shut, towed away and driven into the sea.

Prime Minister May: Are you finished?

M: No. You are. Parliament has made that clear. You're through. It's time to start the dignified exit strategy.

Prime Minister May: Listen to me, you sour-faced boor. I am not going anywhere. Much as it fills my heart with joy to imagine a world without your jarring Essex accent in my ear twelve hours a day, I am not backing down until my deal is accepted.

M: Even after all this tragedy and turmoil, it's somehow endearing you think you have a say in any of this now. Your Nordic poles are virtually materialising in your hands as we speak, begging you to walk away. Boris Johnson - now free of your cabinet and opposed to your deal - is able to paint himself as some sort of hero of the hour. Boris Johnson. Actual Boris 'Cripes Gosh Bim-Bam Whiff-Whaff Union Jack Biddly-Bum' Johnson.

Prime Minister May: You need to breathe.

M: You need to leave.

Prime Minister May: No.

M: I'll send you the exit pack I sent to Cambo.

Prime Minister May: Don't you dare.

M: It's good. It's really useful and I've designed it to be as painless as possible. You won't feel a thing, I promise. Look at Cambo now: fresh-faced, happy, making a fortune on the after-dinner speakers' circuit, plugging his tell-nothing book with Holly and Schofe. That could be you!

Prime Minister May: Do you think I don't talk to David from time to time? He's a lifeless blancmange and you know it. Dead inside. Samantha says he shuts himself in his shepherd's hut for an hour a day just to scream into a pillow.

M: Oh, you were always tougher than that sentient fleece anyway. Listen, I'll send you the exit pack and you can at least—

Prime Minister May: No.

M: Just give it a flick through.

Prime Minister May: Goodbye, Romford.

Prime Minister May hangs up.

AXWORTHY GLOBAL

PO BOX 998 · ALDINGTON ST · KW17 5EH

From: M

To: DJT PR

Date: 01/01/19

Heading: Notes on How POTUS Could Better Present Himself in Interviews Short of Not Turning Up and Hiding in a Golf Bunker with a Fire Bucket on His Head

Message:

In the spirit of wishful thinking, Happy New Year to you all.

It has come to my attention that despite my best efforts to provide advice and guidance on how best to present POTUS in interviews, he still comes across as a disorientated toddler who's just woken up from a nap after a long car journey.

Have *any* of my notes been implemented? From the last few interviews, it seems not. Even *Fox News* can't hide the horror of his catastrophic displays and, let's face it, it is virtually their full-time job to make what is essentially a pushchair with a sloth in it look like the most heroic and intellectual leader the United States has ever produced.

So, can we liaise soon to go over the following points? Because if it carries on like this, the next election result will be a foregone conclusion, or rather it *would* be a foregone conclusion were it not already spectacularly rigged up to its nipples.

1. Can we try to convince POTUS that he needs a new tailor? Specifically, one who doesn't keep getting suits and marquees confused. I saw him shuffle through the West Wing last night, baggy material flapping everywhere. It was like watching a football mascot arrive for a job interview.

2. If he insists on applying this upsettingly cloudy spray tan, can we at least guarantee consistency? The creases around his nostrils always retain an extra layer of spray, so it looks like he's pinched his nose with a KitKat. And can we please do something about his phobia of getting his hands sprayed? His clear white hands look ridiculous against the bronzed hue of his face. Whenever he brings his hands into a close-up it looks like a short, old, white-handed man off-camera is gesturing on his behalf.

3. Please stop him from declaring himself as the best at whatever he's talking about at that particular time. I am aware that his entire personality and presidency is founded on dishonesty (and as a strategy, that's working out well for him) but if he continues to proclaim himself as literally the most knowledgeable man on earth regarding dozens and dozens of subjects, from wind turbines and space travel to medieval history and pet neutering, his supporters are going to become fatigued by his empty posturing. And given that most of his supporters are drugged circus animals, that could

turn out to be the one truly remarkable achievement of his presidency.

Please contact me as soon as you can so we can implement some kind of strategy. And please make sure he doesn't read this memo. Tell him it's about education or climate change.

Thank you. And please order FLOTUS's reinvented Christmas decorations to be taken down now. Those rows of bare white trees in the corridors look like dried-up Tipp-Ex brushes.

- It's amazing how despite saying nothing at all in her latest speech, the PM has made the country loathe her even more than before. That's virtually a magic trick.

- PM wasted a whole day to go to Grimsby to say 'Let's get Brexit done'. Then she came back to London and tweeted a video of herself in Grimsby saying 'Let's get Brexit done'. This is literally the opposite of getting Brexit done. She's such a hopeless plate of moths.

- Watching May on TV tonight insisting her Brexit deal is not dead is like watching a vet put a stethoscope on a sausage.

– The PM is officially the Fyre Festival guy. She spent two years promising a good deal and here we all are sitting in a storm with a cheese sandwich.

– Can't wait for the humanising of the PM after she goes. There'll be a piece in the Telegraph featuring her sporting a new haircut, looking relaxed on a chair in a funky cafe with rustic lightbulbs and the headline will be something like 'I've always been a stubborn old cow'.

AXWORTHY GLOBAL

PO BOX 998 · ALDINGTON ST · KW17 5EH

From: M

To: All @ Axworthy

Date: 16/5/19

Heading: A Guide to the Conservative Party Leadership Contenders

Message:

OK, she's finally done it. She took her damn time but she's finally done it.

Read this and let's get to work. Any queries, call Nikki.

Boris Johnson

Odds: 5/4 favourite

Well, we all know about him. Quite unequivocally driven by status and greed yet somehow has the majority of the Conservative voting public behind him. His rise to the top, despite being a walking shitshow, is worthy of Derren Brown. The only thing that could take this victory away from him is his own fat tongue.

Dominic Raab

Odds: 4/1

Looks like a leader, insofar as to say he has good posture and broad shoulders. He looks good in a suit, like Justin Trudeau. Unfortunately, he's never acted like a leader, nor has he ever said anything worthy of a leader. This man is a drivel machine. A tedious mumbler who can never find a full-stop.

Michael Gove

Odds: 10/1

Believes he can unite the country despite the most prominent stories about him in recent months being his talent for stabbing people in the back. And the front. And then preceding it by saying, 'I am Michael Gove and I am about to stab you in the back and the front.' Probably won't come close to winning because the public see him as untrustworthy, unpleasant, slippery, repugnant, treacherous, wily and devious. The Goveian seven dwarfs.

Andrea Leadsom

Odds: 10/1

The aunt you try to avoid at Christmas because of her 'traditional views'. Might get a rabble of support together due to her unwavering loyalty to deliver Brexit but ultimately she's a figure of fun. Looks like she's more than capable of a couple of potty policies like bringing back tall police helmets or making *Songs of Praise* compulsory in prisons.

Jeremy Hunt

Odds: 12/1

Jeremy Hunt is like the orange crème in a tin of Quality Street. Always there and no one knows why. Less substance than a ghost's burp.

Sajid Javid

Odds: 20/1

Potential to take things to the wire but ultimately will never galvanise the party nor the country because his speeches are as engrossing as a dishwasher cycle.

Rory Stewart

Odds: 25/1

His attempts to speak up for the ordinary person always seem insincere because he's so *Downton Abbey*. You can picture him in a four-poster bed, wearing striped pyjamas and ringing a little bell for Perkins to serve him breakfast. He's the sort of person who would tweet a nice message in support of minority groups and remember to use the right emojis but wouldn't actually do anything about inequality if he were ever in power. His contorted, uncomfortable face looks like it's constantly wrestling with the inner monologue of a colonial major.

Matt Hancock

Odds: 33/1

The more he talks on policies about which he has no expertise, the more apparent it is that his level of success should not have exceeded that of a branch manager of a PC World.

Esther McVey

Odds: 50/1

Esther McVey believes she has the ability to lead the country, which makes me think she's not familiarised herself with herself. Her unkind brand of politics would give her an outside chance were she not jaw-droppingly ignorant on virtually every aspect of modern politics. A small crease to iron out. Maybe next time.

Kit Malthouse

Odds: 100/1

Not sure if he's a real person or not. I've never met him. He sounds like the protagonist in a David Walliams book. Might need to do more research.

Jacob Rees-Mogg

Odds: 1000/1

Jacob Rees-Mogg is what would happen if the ghost of a funeral bell-ringer channelled his death knells from purgatory via the demonic shell of a tortured marionette that had once been hidden up a chimney by an infamous Victorian poisoner. Everyman qualities he has not.

Liz Truss has just called me to rule herself out. I asked her while she was on the phone to also rule herself out of playing scrum half for England in the Rugby World Cup.

On Posh Horse duty again. Big Andrew Neil interview tonight. I don't quite know what Axworthy think I will do. He's going to become leader of the Conservative Party with or without my assistance.

If he spends an hour just throwing forks at Andrew Neil's face this evening, he'll still power his way to victory because there is no credible competition. Jeremy Hunt is the epitome of ineffectuality. If you urgently needed two hundred sandbags to defend your home from flash floods, Jeremy Hunt would turn up three hours later with a multipack of Quavers.

Word at HQ is that Neil is planning to question him on specific points about trade after Brexit, thereby roller-skating him directly into a pyramid of soup cans. So we know what we have to do.

He may be a blundering melon but at least I've trained him to retain facts about trade. Or at the very least filled his head with enough impenetrable trade-related terms that he'll just confuse anyone who speaks to him and they'll have no option but to move on.

As I have conveyed to him in the past, if all else fails just turn your scrambled thoughts into an audible geyser of incredulous guff. It's impossible for any human (even Andrew Neil, whom I understand has a soul behind those librarian's glasses) to endure more than three minutes of him when he's clumsily garbling towards a point he never reaches.

Should be plain sailing.

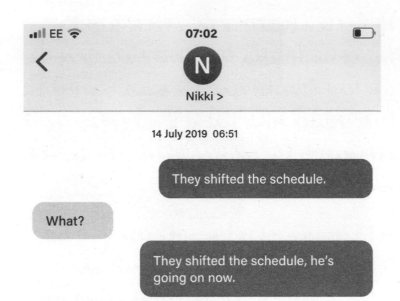

14 July 2019 06:51

> They shifted the schedule.

What?

> They shifted the schedule, he's going on now.

Now? Oh. Well, we're ready, aren't we? We've done all the prep, we've drummed the answers into him, what could go wrong?

> GATT 24 Paragraph 5B.

GATT what?

> I'm hearing Andrew Neil is planning to trip him up over GATT 24 Paragraph 5B.

Oh.

You see, that 'oh' suggests you didn't put anything in his notes about GATT 24 Paragraph 5B.

Well . . .

And that 'well' confirms it. Thank you so much. We're toast. We're buttered toast and sodding jam.

Hold on a second, what is GATT 24 Paragraph 5B?

If I knew that I wouldn't be calling you, would I? But thanks for making this chat doubly pointless.

Where are you now?

I just had to go out of the building to make a call because I can't get a signal in the BBC newsroom, which by the way I find incredibly suspect. I bet Jeremy Corbyn's battered Nokia works in the BBC newsroom.

Questions Over Hidden Earpiece as Johnson Flounders in Interview

17 July 2019

Conservative leadership frontrunner Boris Johnson has admitted in an interview with the BBC's Andrew Neil that he is unfamiliar with a specific and important detail in his plan for a no-deal Brexit.

Citing paragraph 5(b) of Article 24 of the General Agreement on Tariffs and Trade (GATT), of the World Trade Organization, Mr Johnson tried to allay fears that Britain would be plunged into economic disaster if it left on October 31st without a deal. But when Mr Neil brought up the need to address paragraph 5(c), Mr Johnson looked stunned and sheepish, and hesitated as if he were expecting someone else to relay the answer to him.

At this point, a tinny voice could also be heard berating Mr Johnson, calling him a 'stupid sausage roll' and comparing him to a 'supermarket trolley of perished lettuce', leading some people to believe that he was being fed answers by an adviser.

This is not the first time that Mr Johnson has been accused of concealing an earpiece for a public appearance. Richard Compton, former cabinet adviser and now a digital communications expert, has suggested that the technique is prevalent throughout British politics. 'I've seen it many times, across the political spectrum. It seems no one in public office these days can be expected to enter the arena alone. It's almost impossible for a politician or a public figure now to convey their thoughts and feelings without regimented assistance.'

Mr Compton also believes that the phenomenon goes further. 'I've heard unconfirmed rumours that an apolitical organisation is actually hired to advise public figures on both ends of the spectrum this way. Without wishing to sound dramatic, the political narrative in this country could well be controlled by a mysterious cabal who are driven only by profit and about whom we know nothing,' he said dramatically.

When asked about the latest incident, which mistakenly recorded the raised voice of Mr Johnson's adviser calling his employer a 'boiled egg of incompetence', Mr Compton replied, 'I find it wholly shocking not only that the future leader of this country cannot answer questions about trade without prompting but also that somebody somewhere has the authority to call him – without fear of recrimination – a "vase of wank".'

AXWORTHY GLOBAL

PO BOX 998 · ALDINGTON ST · KW17 5EH

From: M

To: A

Date: 18/07/19

Heading: The *Independent* newspaper article headed 'Questions Over Hidden Earpiece as Johnson Flounders in Interview'

Message:

I must apologise for causing further speculation as to the existence of Axworthy in the national press. I am aware that our organisation's anonymity is paramount and it troubles me greatly to think that my lack of professionalism has brought about more thoughtless and dangerous conjecture.

With regards to the incident, I take full responsibility. I raised my voice and used unforgivable language as I tried to salvage what I could from the interview.

As a result, the focus shifted away from the message and onto me, and I cannot defend breaking a rule so embedded in the prestigious history of Axworthy.

However, I hope you will understand that to advise Boris Johnson is like telling a toddler to put his shoes on. He doesn't so much answer a question as shuffle around it haphazardly like a laboratory mouse who prefers to get lost in the maze rather than search for the cheese.

My patience got the better of me and I snapped. It should not have happened. But in my defence the political landscape is changing rapidly and I'm having to develop my style to accommodate these new personalities. And when I say the political landscape is changing I mean there are more people in office now with the sensibilities of hornets than there were before.

Yes, Bush and Blair gave us a world of pain. But it was a world of pain we could control. With morphine. I guess that's the problem. There's no morphine any more. Nothing to relieve the agony. Occasionally we'll get a quick burst from a nasal spray but that's about it.

Sorry, I appear to have wandered off on a tangent. That's what comes from spending time with Boris Johnson.

Anyway, I will do my best to adapt, rapidly.

Thank you.

M.

19 July 2019 07:04

I need a dead cat and I need it now.

You need a pet cemetery.

Uncalled for.

Something interesting came in from our sources at Westminster this morning.

Go on.

Are you aware of Gregory Feldman?

Formerly Secretary of State for Transport, now a fairly ineffectual backbencher.

That's right, spends most of his time these days being knocked out in the first round of television cookery contests.

What about him?

It's been known for years that he's a serial Webipedia-tinkerer.

His or other people's?

Mainly his, though he has been known to amend others. He got into trouble for claiming Baroness Warsi was addicted to online bingo and that Iain Duncan Smith has a forked tongue. But in the last 24 hours he's changed his own page a dozen times and our people have counted seven fabrications among them.

Why?

It seems very much like he's flipped his melon. Before this happened, he'd been scrutinised in the press over another matter and friends say he's close to breaking point.

Well, he shouldn't have gone into politics.

No, this was about failing to make his chicken and leek puff pie rise on Celebrity Pastry Chefs.

His what on what?

I'll send a screengrab of Feldman's Webipedia page with all his changes highlighted, then we can leak it to the press.

Celebrity what?

Home page

Contents

Articles

Random events

About Webipedia

Contribute

Donate

Upload file

Community forum

Upload

Help

Tools

Links

Special links

Page information

Output

Print

Export

Download

✏ Edit links

Gregory Feldman

From Webipedia, the free encyclopedia

Gregory Feldman (born 14 September 1968) is a British politician and member of the Conservative Party. He has been the Member of Parliament (MP) for Plyfield Bovering since the 2005 general election. Following the 2010 general election, he was appointed Secretary of State for Transport. On 28 November 2015, he stood down from his ministerial position due to the refusal of Parliament to acquiesce to Feldman's demand that his pet tortoise Cynthia accompany him to all cabinet meetings. 'Any vet will tell you a tortoise is the most therapeutic animal. Along with dogs, dolphins and some sea lions.'

Family and early life [edit]

Feldman was born in Hocklington, Herefordshire. He was educated at St Keith's Primary School, 'Watford Grammar School for Boys and Occasional Girls' and Little Wellies Agricultural College.

Political career [edit]

Shadow housing minister [edit]

In June 2007, Feldman became shadow housing minister. During this period of opposition, he argued in favour of the building of large houses instead of small ones, proposed that to save money on materials all bricks should be cube-shaped instead of oblong and that houses should be built with the side facing out because 'the side of a house is the best part'.

Secretary of State for the Home Department [edit]

For the period of time between 2.34 p.m. and 3.57 p.m. on 8 November 2014, Feldman was Secretary of State for the Home Department due to a computer error. The computer was rebooted and Feldman was relieved of his duties. 'I've got to know some great people here but it's time to move on and face fresh new challenges,' he said.

Denials of second job [edit]

Feldman has long denied having a second job while being an MP. In February 2015 he told LBC Radio, 'I have never had a second job while acting as MP and I will never have a second job as an MP. These are scurrilous lies. The idea of me taking a second job is absurd. Preposterous. Second job. Honestly. Ridiculous.'

In March 2015 Feldman admitted having a second job and later stated that during the LBC interview he made a mistake saying otherwise, because at that time he didn't 'have all the facts' about himself.

Allegations of Webipedia editing [edit]

In 2012 the *Guardian* reported that Feldman had been regularly tampering with his Webipedia entry, removing facts and replacing them with completely spurious sentences. Webipedia founder Timmy Bales, who writes all the entries himself, said, 'I can't see anything wrong. Now would you please leave me alone, I'm halfway through an 8,000-word entry about the Baltic Sea.'

AXWORTHY GLOBAL

PO BOX 998 · ALDINGTON ST · KW17 5EH

From: M

To: All @ Axworthy

Date: 23/07/19

Heading: The Pocketbook

Message:

First of all, let me say how flattered I am that one of you went to all the trouble of compiling this pocketbook to herald the beginning of Boris Johnson's tenure as Prime Minister of Great Britain and Northern Ireland.

To know that my words are being examined and compiled in this manner makes me feel as if I'm being elevated to some sort of iconic status within the organisation. It's tremendously humbling.

Second, when I find out which one of you did it, I will not only have you dropped from your post, I shall also render you unemployable for the rest of your life. Seriously. Your identity and achievements will be erased. The following week you will possess neither the skills nor the qualifications to operate the bubble machine in Hamleys.

Now, I enjoy a good laugh as much as anyone. (Not that I can remember having a good laugh in the last ten years. I think I watched a film once that had a funny bit in it. I want to say *Men in Black III*, maybe? But that's about it.) However, when I found that the direct line from my room mic had been intercepted by someone in the office to make their own private recordings, I was not laughing.

It has been made clear to me that the interceptions were made because the perpetrator in question is a 'fan' and wanted not only to keep my conversations with public figures for his/her own private record but to also make an A–Z pocketbook of my insults for a limited publication to be distributed among other members of the organisation.

In many ways my heart is warmed by your refusal as a team to name this person. After all, solidarity is paramount here at Axworthy. But on the other hand, if you don't tell me who did this soon, I'm going to sack you all and replace you with those robots that walk like dogs.

You have 48 hours.

Best,

M.

B

Bag of flour
Bag of flutes
Barbaric fart
Basket of nothing
Baffling horse
Beige shirt
Belligerent chop
Blazing ninny
Blustering bigot
Bowl of sugar
Bubonic trolley
Brainless wasp
Brass-bottomed clodpole
Bumbling plop
Bumptious hat
Bungling valve

218

C

Cacophonous fop
Catastrophic hornet
Cardboard sod
Careless manbag
Carpeted toilet
Ceramic turd
Certified pudding
Chaotic bin
Chaotic bun
(Total) chimney
Ceremonial pony
Clammy worm
Clattering basket
Clueless flask of poisonous burps
(Hopeless) cobweb
Cretaceous omelette

219

D

Daft egg
Dangerous puffin
Dank meme
Deplorable onion
Despotic mop
Digestive biscuit
Dishwasher tablet
Dizzy otter
Doughy clanger
Dozy fishfinger
Dreadful boil
Dreary flannel
Drippy squirrel
Drunk blobfish
Duplicitous nozzle
(Pointless) duvet

220

M

Malicious bumbag
Marble prune
Mealy-mouthed spider
Meandering melon
Meaningless button
Mephitic shoehorn
Metallic thumb
Meteoric numpty
Massive sausage
Miserable flan
Miserable sock
Monstrous flummery
Mortifying gannet
(Absolute) moth
Myopic meringue

229

AXWORTHY GLOBAL

PO BOX 998 · ALDINGTON ST · KW17 5EH

From: M

To: Prime Minister Johnson

Date: 15/09/2019

Heading: Choice of words

Message:

Prime Minister,

I have it on good authority that you have just compared yourself to the Hulk, for 'throwing off the shackles of the EU'.

May I suggest that a more accurate reason for calling yourself the Hulk is because you're irrational, destructive and always in need of a tailor.

I understand that, with May gone, you've been keen over the last few months to assert yourself and your new government as a powerful force of intimidation and ruthlessness – 'get Brexit done' and all that – but if your policies are a family-sized bargain bucket of half-cooked ideas that no one believes, then what are you really? You're not the Hulk. You're barely a sidekick in the Marvel universe. You're not even that arrow guy.

Stop pulling up your trousers by the belt and giving it the pig-headed tough guy approach just because your chief aide told you to – who, by the way, looks about as tough as a tortoise with food poisoning. It's not working. Everyone knows you're going to have to cave in to the demands being put upon you by the European Parliament, the British Parliament and now the Supreme Court. It's time to hold your hands up and say you got the Brexit strategy wrong.

Saying you got something wrong is not a sign of weakness. In any other walk of life, changing your mind about something is not a big deal, but in party politics it's the most sinful course of action. Why? It's so ridiculously immature and symptomatic of male bravado. Imagine you're cycling through London and someone throws a mat of spikes across your cycle lane. Would you stop, change direction and choose another route? Or would you just plough right through it in case your peers accused you of dithering? Being too flaky? Too wishy-washy? Lacking faith. Lacking determination. Lackling good old-fashioned British steel!

There's 'being determined' and there's 'your arse in a pyramid of rubbish bags with a punctured wheel bouncing off down the road'.

And on top of this, you think the best way to distract everyone from your spectacular blunders this week is to bring up your stupid notion of a bridge across the Irish Sea. Will you stop it with this bloody bridge? You're like Trump and his wall, except of course his wall is a very real symbol of division and hatred. Ironically, your bridge is just a diversion.

£15 billion it would cost. I could think of 15 billion better examples of where that money could go, you cretinous out-of-touch plop. Mind you, £15 billion is the figure *you* put on it – not a bridge engineer or a leading firm of architects – YOU:

a failed journalist. Keep on this self-destructive path, mate, and there's only one place your premiership will take you, and it's going to make the Irish Sea feel like a paddling pool.

Pack it in, arrow guy. Just pack it in.

Best,

M.

BORIS JOHNSON'S UN SPEECH (WITH AMENDMENTS), 25TH SEPTEMBER 2019

Mr President, Your Excellencies, Ladies and Gentlemen, faithful late night (audience.)

Why are you doing this speech at midnight btw? Who has ever said they prefer you to a comfortable bed? Actually, don't answer that.

It is customary for the British Prime Minister to come to this United Nations and pledge to advance our values and defend our rules, the rules of a peaceful (world.)

It's also customary to be brief when you're on at midnight so cut this bit please.

From protecting freedom of navigation in the Gulf

To persevering in the vital task of achieving a two-state solution to the conflict in the Middle East.

And of course I am proud to do all of these (things.) *All these two things?*

But no one can ignore a gathering force that is reshaping the future of every member of this Assembly.

There has been nothing like it in history

When I think of the great scientific revolutions of the past – print, the steam engine, aviation, the atomic age – I think of new tools that we acquired but over which we – the human race – had the (advantage.) *Like zipwires?*

Which we (controlled.) *Like zipwires?*

That is not necessarily the case in the (digital age.)

I know you're scared of the digital age but honestly no one else is. This is all because of that dream you had about the sentient fridge that sounded like Jeremy Corbyn.

You may keep secrets from your friends, from your parents, your children, your doctor – even your personal (trainer) – but it takes real effort to conceal your thoughts from (Google.)

Yeah, I wouldn't leav a big gap for laughter here.

You sound so sweet when you reference something modern, like a drunk Edwardian bishop trying to work an espresso machine.

And if that is true today, in future there may be nowhere to (hide.) *Except a zipwire?*

Smart cities will pullulate with sensors, all joined together by the 'internet of (things), bollards communing invisibly with lamp (posts)

Are you well?

If any sentence in this speech shows you have no grasp of what you're talking about it's surely 'the internet of things'.

So there is always a parking space for your electric car,

so that no bin goes unemptied, no street unswept

and the urban environment is as antiseptic as a (Zurich) (pharmacy.)

Why Zurich? Why pharmacy? Actually just why?

But this technology could also be used to keep every citizen under round-the-clock (surveillance.) *Oh now I see why this bothers you.*

A future Alexa will pretend to take orders.

But this Alexa will be watching you,

An Alexa with a tongue and feet is perhaps the most horrifying image you've conjured up in my mind and believe me you've planted a few.

Clucking her tongue and stamping her (foot.)

In the future, voice connectivity will be in every room
and almost every object:

Even less evidence of this. Are you trying to be funny? Is this your idea of humour?

No evidence of this.

your mattress will monitor your (nightmares) your fridge
will beep for more (cheese;)

Your personality is so confusing at times, it's like trying to decipher a war code. But a deeply uninteresting, pointless one.

your front door will sweep wide the moment you
approach, like some silent (butler;) your smart meter will
go hustling – of its accord – for the cheapest electricity.

Doors don't open LIKE butlers, doors are opened BY butlers but honestly this is the most coherent thing you've said so far, so keep it in.

And every one of them minutely transcribing your every
habit in tiny electronic shorthand,

Stored not in their chips or their (innards) – nowhere you
can find it,

Why does your choice of words always make me nauseous?

But in some great cloud of data that lours ever more
oppressively over the human (race)

You think it's really a cloud, don't you?

A giant dark (thundercloud) *You do, don't you?*

waiting to burst

And we have no control over how or when the
precipitation will take (place) *Yeah you do, okay.*

And every day that we tap on our phones or work on our
iPads – as I see some of you doing now – *They're all trying to get an Uber, trust me.*

We not only leave our indelible spoor in the ether *Nauseous again.*

But we are ourselves becoming a resource

Click by click, tap by tap.

Just as the carboniferous period created the indescribable
wealth – leaf by decaying leaf – of hydrocarbons. *Keeping it light for the midnight audience, cool.*

Data is the crude oil of the modern economy

And we are now in an environment where

We don't know who should own these new oil fields

We don't always know who should have the rights or the
title to these gushers of cash *Really becoming quite ill now.*

And we don't know who decides how to use that data.

Can these algorithms be trusted with our lives and hopes? *As opposed to you? Sure.*

Should the machines – and only the machines – decide
whether or not we are eligible for a mortgage or
insurance *I don't know but that's one boring 'Terminator' film.*

Or what surgery or medicines we should receive?

Are we doomed to a cold and heartless future in which
computer says yes – or computer says no

With the grim finality of an emperor in the arena?

How do you plead with an (algorithm?) How do you get *This is just turning into awful sixth-former poetry now.*
it to see the extenuating circumstances?

The reason I am giving this speech today is that the *Are you seriously trying to convince*
UK is one of the world's tech leaders — and I believe *the UN you're*
governments have been simply caught unawares by the *on the ball with*
unintended consequences of the (internet;) *technological innovation?*
You still have your
AI – what will it mean? *Blockbuster membership card.*

Helpful robots washing and caring for an ageing
(population) *Washing? Seriously? That's the number one priority for you with regards to AI? Being given a wash by a robot?*

or pink-eyed terminators sent back from the future to
cull the human (race?) *Can they start with you?*

What will synthetic biology stand for — restoring our *How drunk have*
livers and our eyes with miracle regeneration of the *you been that you've*
tissues, like some fantastic hangover (cure?) *needed new eyes in the morning?*

Or will it bring terrifying limbless chickens to our (tables?)
I just want you to know I've stabbed myself in the leg with this pen.

Will nanotechnology help us to beat disease, or will it leave
tiny robots to replicate in the (crevices) of our cells?
Yep, nauseous again.

It is a trope as old as literature that any scientific advance is punished by the (gods.) *Oh shit, here we go. 'I read Classics one afternoon in 1983 so here's fifteen minutes of wank about Agamemnon.'*

When Prometheus brought fire to (mankind) *Oh man, can we go back to limbless chickens?*

In a tube of fennel, as you may (remember,) Zeus punished *Oh yes, we all* him by chaining him to a tartarean crag while his liver *remember that,* was pecked out by an eagle *the fire in a tube of fucking fennel, yes I was reading it only yesterday in my library, you absolute horsefart.*

And every time his liver re-grew the eagle came back and pecked it again

And this went on for ever – a bit like the experience of *I explicitly said* (Brexit) in the UK, if some of our parliamentarians had *not to mention* their way. *it tonight, you flump.*

Success will depend, now as ever, on freedom, openness and pluralism,

the formula that not only emancipates the human spirit, *I'm too angry* but releases the boundless ingenuity and inventiveness of *to make notes* (mankind,) *now. I'm going back to my hotel room. To be washed by a robot.*

and which, above all, the United Kingdom will strive to preserve and advance.

Excellencies, Ladies and Gentlemen, thank you for your kind attention.

AXWORTHY GLOBAL

PO BOX 998 · ALDINGTON ST · KW17 5EH

13 November 2019

HRH Prince Andrew
Royal Lodge Windsor
Windsor Great Park
Berkshire

Your Royal Highness,

Thank you for giving me the opportunity to provide you with
assistance for the forthcoming interview on *Newsnight*. Emily Maitlis
has a stare that could melt the door off a casino vault so you're going
to need to go into that meeting with your best warpaint on.

Here's what she may ask and how you should answer it:

- Why did you go to a party given by Jeffrey Epstein,
  celebrating his release?

  *Say something like: 'It was a <u>dinner</u> party. Very different thing.
  In fact, I'm not sure if I've ever been to a party without dinner.
  Sounds like a wasted opportunity, if you ask me!' (Perhaps a
  chuckle here to get Emily on side.)*

- Why did you think Jeffrey Epstein's house was a convenient
  place to stay?

  *You'll need to acknowledge that a convenient place to stay is the
  Crowne Plaza or the Holiday Inn or literally anywhere else other
  than a paedophile's house. And don't talk about the 'benefits
  of hindsight', which I know is a favourite excuse of yours. The
  fact is you don't need hindsight not to stay in a convicted sex
  offender's house. Just regular sight would have done.*

- Why do you defend your friendship with Jeffrey Epstein even now?

  It's time to admit that you regret ever knowing him. I know he introduced you to a lot of influential people but here's why that doesn't work as an explanation:

  a) *You are literally a prince. Your mother is the queen. She's on all the money and the stamps. You're a bit influential yourself, no? And who exactly are these 'influential people' you talk of who couldn't be reached through the normal channels like say via an invitation to a garden party or the launching of a ship or something?*

  b) *You're basically saying sex traffickers are great for networking, which I'm afraid isn't what I'd call 'playing the sympathy vote'.*

- Virginia Giuffre alleges Epstein sent her to you to spend the evening together at Tramp nightclub.

  Straight off the bat, you're going to have to deny this. Yes, you went to Tramp but it was never to have a good time.

- Virginia Giuffre remembers dancing with you and that you sweated profusely.

  Again, blanket denial here. This may be a bit of a stretch, but I think you should say that you didn't sweat at the time because of a medical condition that stops your sweat glands from producing sweat. The tactic here is that Emily Maitlis won't be able to deal with your wobbly chops talking in detail about sweat glands and may change the subject swiftly to stop herself boaking.

  If you're pressed on this medical condition, however, tell Emily that it came about via an overdose of adrenaline that you experienced during some stressful event in your life. Now, being an obsolete prince with zero chance of throne action, one would imagine that the most stressful event you've ever had to deal with is when you were snowed in at a ski resort and were forced to eat a Pot Noodle, but do rack your brains to think of any traumatic moments we could use. I've made a list below to which you might like to add some more examples.

- *Fighting in the Falklands War*
- *Riding the Corkscrew rollercoaster at Alton Towers*
- *Participating in the royal episode of* It's A Knockout
- *Dealing with a pigeon that's flown into the kitchen*
- *Worrying about the Millennium Bug*
- *The time you had to make a slice of toast by yourself and nearly burned down Windsor Castle*
- *When a rat escaped on the day that a hotel inspector paid a visit*
- *When a guest died and you had to smuggle the body out of the hotel*
- *When you insulted some German guests after being hit on the head by a— Oh wait, sorry, the last three suggestions are episodes of* Fawlty Towers. *Ignore those.*

Looking forward to seeing you tomorrow. I'm sure you'll do fine. Don't sweat it(!)

Best,

M.

From: M [mailto: m@axworthy.com]
To: no10-communications@gov.org.uk
Date: 19th November 2019
Subject: Despicable, Despicable Shits

Well, I'm not going to beat around the bush here. That trick you pulled last night was the most shameful piece of skullfuckery I've ever witnessed in all my years in this wretched position.

Rebranding the official Conservative HQ Twitter account as 'factcheckUK' during the televised leaders' debate and pushing anti-opposition messages was nothing but a malicious and calculated Harry Potter shitspell designed to mislead and befuddle. And let me tell you, heads will roll for it.

Not only has this wholly unnecessary episode caused much consternation amongst media outlets across the political spectrum, but it has also triggered a couple of journalists into resurrecting their investigations into Axworthy. The view is that such a shameful piece of underhanded *and* cack-handed plotting could *surely* only have been implemented by an outside source.

That's what really pisses me off. They think *we* were responsible for this. We've come so close to being exposed the last couple of years and if it is this nonsense that brings us down, I swear to God I'm going to be taking down as many of you with me as possible. My hands will be gripped on Michael Gove's bony wrist like a diver's watch, trust me.

Fix this now, you loathsome Oxbridge fox turds. The election's not won yet.

Best,

M.

Diary: Thursday 12th December 2019

Five more years.

Five. More. Years.

Earlier this evening I worked out how old I'll be at the next election. I had to sit down.

I'm currently at the foot of the stairs, unable to move.

By all accounts, the journalistic investigations into the existence of Axworthy continue, the Trump impeachment is imminent, and a powerful, menacing Conservative government has just been re-elected with a toxic sponge cake at the helm...

Part of me hopes the investigations into us bear fruit, because I don't know how much longer I can do this job. Every day I have to climb the Eiffel Tower and every day they grease it just a little more.

18 December 2019 00.04

> Mr President, it's M. This is my
> anonymous Twitter handle. I need to
> speak with you.

Curtis Poll @CurtisInside

> Your through. Your WHOLE
> ORGANISATION is through. Your
> not supposed to let this kind of
> SHIT happen!

Donald J. Trump @realDonaldTrump

> *You're. It was never our job to
> obstruct justice. That was your job.
> Our job was to steer you on a path
> where you might be able to lead the
> country slightly better than a dog
> with an oven glove on its head. I am
> willing to accept that we failed in that
> respect.

Curtis Poll @CurtisInside

> 'Look at me I'm Mr Cockney
> Earpiece Know-Nothing. I hide in
> a room all day sucking my thumb
> while my boss takes the HEAT for
> EVERYTHING.' Your a JOKE. Your
> THROUGH!

Donald J. Trump @realDonaldTrump

You need us, Mr President. You need us for what's about to come.

Curtis Poll @CurtisInside

Donald Trump doesn't NEED ANYBODY. Donald Trump is the PRESIDENT OF THE UNITED STATES! AMERICA!

Donald J. Trump @realDonaldTrump

Can you try and talk to me rather than hitting the keys with your fist and letting autocorrect finish your thoughts?

Curtis Poll @CurtisInside

You're SAD PAL. A sad little man working for an organisation that's going DOWN THE TUBES. Everyone's saying it. In a YEAR'S TIME EVERYONE WILL KNOW WHO YOU ARE AND WHAT YOU DO! And you know where I'll be?

Donald J. Trump @realDonaldTrump

In jail?

Curtis Poll @CurtisInside

Serving a glorious SECOND TERM! This impeachment is a WITCH HUNT and I'm gonna DEFEAT IT!

Donald J. Trump @realDonaldTrump

You're not familiar with how witch hunts worked out by and large, are you?

Curtis Poll @CurtisInside

I know more than YOU. I know MORE THAN ANYBODY.

Donald J. Trump @realDonaldTrump

With all due respect, I've emptied the contents of my food tray at McDonald's into receptacles with a greater understanding of the world than you.

Curtis Poll @CurtisInside

You can insult me all you want . . .

Donald J. Trump @realDonaldTrump

Cool, thanks.

Curtis Poll @CurtisInside

. . . because soon you will no longer have your organisation to PROTECT YOU. Axworthy is FINISHED. And without AXWORTHY your just a LOSER IN A ROOM, pal. You may even end up in JAIL!

Donald J. Trump @realDonaldTrump

Well, as ever, this has been a hugely beneficial discourse and not at all a waste of my time. Good luck with the impeachment.

Curtis Poll @CurtisInside

Donald Trump doesn't NEED LUCK. Donald Trump KNOWS THE SYSTEM AND WILL BEAT IT! AMERICA!

Donald J. Trump @realDonaldTrump

I must say I really thought that the concept of justice would be a permanent fixture in our society, not something to be discarded and then looked back on with nostalgic fondness years later as if it were a children's TV show or a pair of mom jeans.

Curtis Poll @CurtisInside

What are you TALKING about?! SAD. Blocking you. BYE LOSER.

Donald J. Trump @realDonaldTrump

Goodbye, Mr President.

Curtis Poll @CurtisInside

AXWORTHY GLOBAL

PO BOX 998 · ALDINGTON ST · KW17 5EH

[20 December 2019]

[Bundeskanzleramt
Bundeskanzlerin
Angela Merkel
Willy-Brandt-Straße 1
10557 Berlin]

[Dear Chancellor Merkel],

I am writing to offer my advice and guidance as a political adviser.

Now, I am not for one moment suggesting that the way in which you conduct yourself in the public eye is falling dangerously below expectations. However, it would be churlish of me not to extend an invitation to you to become part of the ever growing number of heads of state throughout the world who have agreed to house me firmly in their ear.

So why should you hire me and remove all other advisers from your realm? Well, put simply, I'm the best out there. I was able to convince the British electorate that Boris Johnson was suitable to lead the country when, in reality, he should be as far removed from any position of power as it is possible to be without needing an oxygen tank.

If I can make someone like Johnson (whose responsibilities in life should have been limited to – at the very most – managing a chaotic and right-leaning second-hand bookshop in Tunbridge

Wells) rise to the position of prime minister, think what I can do for you – someone who actually functions as a human being. The possibilities are endless!

Please do get in touch as soon as you can. I am a great admirer of what you have achieved. In fact my admiration goes back to the beginning of your career. I was there for the gigs when you were just starting out. Those early speeches on electoral reform blew my socks off. The energy was electric in those pub basements. [NB: replace these details on a leader-specific basis.] I even had a poster of you on my wall. Well, not a poster as such. It was just a really big leaflet. But it still worked.

You were an inspiration to me in my early years. Well, you and Morrissey. And now that the young, hopeful, enigmatic lead singer of The Smiths is now just a sweaty fascist who occasionally burps unpleasantries on stage like an uncle at a wedding, you're all I've got.

I would consider it an honour to be part of your next political campaign. And it would almost certainly be a privilege for you too.

Yours sincerely,

M.

New letter template to entice leaders who have resisted offers of our help thus far. A-Merk is just an example. Might come in handy if POTUS pulls the plug.

AXWORTHY GLOBAL

PO BOX 998 · ALDINGTON ST · KW17 5EH

23 January 2020

The Right Honourable Boris Johnson
10 Downing Street
Westminster
London SW1A 2AA

Dear Prime Minister,

I am writing to you in the strictest confidence and as a matter of urgency.

As you know I am currently in Beijing with Liz Truss negotiating trade deals with China. I won't divulge too much about what is being discussed, as we're at a very delicate point in the negotiations, but suffice to say you'll be lucky if she comes home with her luggage.

Anyway, there's a lot of talk in China about this so-called 'coronavirus' at the moment and I wanted to make sure that we're setting up all the necessary safeguards back in the UK.

I believe there are now five confirmed cases in Britain so it's imperative we do what we can now to stop this virus spreading in exactly the same way that it is over here in China. With that in mind I believe our most pressing matter is the removal of the Health Secretary, Matt Hancock. Seriously, he needs to be dropped faster than Kevin Spacey.

I have always been used to prime ministers rewarding loyal colleagues with important cabinet positions. It's a frankly disgraceful tradition because it's the responsibility of our leaders to appoint the people best suited to the roles in question, not to divvy them out like After Eight mints to favoured MPs just because they stood by them the last time their head was on the chopping block. However, I'm aware that this is the rule and not even Axworthy can change it. Hence Matt Hancock.

You and I both know that Matt Hancock is the Health Secretary because he had your back. He ruled himself out of the leadership contest early and threw his weight behind you. And that is why the Member of Parliament for West Suffolk – an economist with a not-at-all-exceptional background in software and the housing market – is in charge of the National Health Service of the United Kingdom. It's terrifying, really. But I'm not here to bleat about injustices under your administration. If that were the case, I'd need to put 250 more sheets of A4 in the printer tray.

I implore you to shuffle Hancock somewhere else in the cabinet. In the event that the virus becomes a major threat to this country, he simply would not have the capacity to deal with such an extraordinary event; he doesn't really have the capacity to take a shirt back to Topman and ask for a refund without breaking into a sweat and falling into a basket of socks.

If the virus reaches the kind of levels we're seeing here in China, he will be required to give daily press briefings. Daily press briefings. Matt Hancock. This is a man who needs a minimum of 20 umms when he's ordering a coffee.

Ordinarily I wouldn't mind Matt Hancock being Health Secretary if I knew that the government collectively were capable of dealing with this sort of emergency. Forgive my bluntness, Prime Minister, but I do not believe that to be the case. In fact, I'm so fearful of the mistakes you would make during a pandemic that I'm going to bed on a full bottle of red every night.

Therefore the idea of putting Matt Hancock up at the podium on a daily basis to make a pig's ear of defending the government for making a pig's ear of containing the virus is scaring the bobbins out of me.

Please can we schedule a meeting at some point to ensure this matter does not spiral out of control?

Please.

Best,

M.

P.S. I see you've been invited to attend a COBRA meeting tomorrow, perhaps we can catch up after that?

AXWORTHY GLOBAL

PO BOX 998 · ALDINGTON ST · KW17 5EH

From: M

To: All @ DowningStComms

Date: 03/02/2020

Heading: Brexit Bash

Message:

Hello, team. Thanks for your invitation to the Downing Street party to celebrate Britain leaving the EU. I hear all canapés will be sourced from Britain! Nice one. Very clever. My mouth is watering at the thought of all those tiny gravy-soaked Yorkshire puddings being passed around the country's most fervent Brexiteers.

Sadly I won't be able to make it because I'll be lying face down in my garden at midnight, screaming into the lawn.

Please find my invitation stapled to the bottom of this document with a few suggestions as to how it could be improved.

Best,

M.

You are invited to a Celebration of Britain

at No. 10 Downing Street on
Thursday 13th February 2020 at 9 p.m.

To mark the occasion of the United Kingdom leaving the European Union and embracing the (new) (opportunities) that lie ahead, Prime Minister Boris Johnson is hosting a celebration of Britain at No. 10 Downing Street and would be greatly enthused by your (presence.)

Canapés will be sourced from Britain alone and will include such culinary delights as savoury shortbread topped with Shropshire blue cheese, a ploughman's lunch of cheddar and pickle, and roast beef and Yorkshire pudding with a horseradish sauce.

Please respond as soon as possible to the Downing Street Communications (Team.)

We look forward to your company.

Cool, yes never mind running the press office of the leader of the country with any degree of competence – we've got fifty rosy-cheeked middle-aged men to fill up with British pickle!

The only thing that would greatly enthuse me would b[e] if guests were permitted to pelt his drowsy dog-like fac[e] with fistfuls of Shropshire blue cheese.

6 February 2020 06:03

Jacob Rees-Mogg is doing some media interviews this morning about the coronavirus and wants a few pointers.

What is JRM doing giving media interviews about the coronavirus?

PM's orders.

We can't have that streak of spider poison talk about coronavirus. That's as reassuring as having Pennywise the Clown home-school your children. Plus he's largely uninformed about anything that occurred after 1850.

Look, he's going on 5Live in half an hour so can you just send him something please.

Sure.

Jacob Rees-Mogg's Guide to Stop Coronavirus Spreading

– keep opium in your snuffbox
– always have a leech handy
– take 60 drops of laudanum before vespers
– medicated vapours on the morrow after the sabbath
– cocaine and bed

Great. Thanks. No, really.

No probs.

Coronavirus Spreads Through Italy as Hancock Fails to Keep His Cards Close to His Chest

Matt Hancock Writes Himself a Pep Talk on Cards Before Briefing on Virus

26th February 2020

In a press conference at Downing Street today, the Health Secretary Matt Hancock announced that the government would be launching a mass public information campaign giving advice on how to safeguard against the coronavirus.

However, his announcement soon became the second story this afternoon when an eagle-eyed photographer spotted that he was clutching half a dozen cards upon which were written a number of short, encouraging sentences.

The sentences, seemingly written by Mr Hancock, made a series of very brief proclamations such as 'You've got this', 'Don't listen to him' and 'You're simply the best (better than all the rest)'.

Westminster tongues have been wagging furiously over the 'Don't listen to him' card in particular. Labour MP Greg Morgan said,

'Everyone here is wondering who the subject of the card is, and why "he" *shouldn't* be listened to. It's all very intriguing.'

Mr Hancock's announcement that there have been 13 cases of the virus in the UK so far fell by the wayside as speculation increased about his self-penned pep talk, which he felt the need to refer to on multiple occasions during the press conference.

As Mr Hancock listed the number of countries to report their first cases, including Austria, Croatia, Switzerland, France, Norway, Greece and South America, theories were being circulated as to who could have driven the Health Secretary to such bizarre self-soothing measures.

A Whitehall source poured cold water on the idea that it could have been in reference to Boris Johnson's chief aide Dominic Cummings. 'It's not Dom. Dom may look like a *Star Wars* villain but in all honesty he lacks the true menace to unsettle anyone. That's a fact. He's a spineless misfit essentially. No, I think this is someone with real influence.'

Over the last few years there have been a number of rumours throughout Westminster that some sort of covert organisation has been brought in to assist with the public relations of the government, though no one at Number 10 has ever commented on the matter. It is also believed that the same organisation has been deployed to support President Trump.

'Everyone knows the rumours,' the Whitehall source explained. 'It's just no one knows anything tangible. But trust me – whoever they are, they've got to Matt, and he's hurting. He looked like an injured My Little Pony up there.'

From: M [mailto: m@axworthy.com]
Sent: 3rd March 2020 18:31
To: Chris Whitty [mailto: cwhitty@gov.uk]
Subject: Shaking Hands

Chris,

I know what you're going to say. But you can't blame me for what happened today. I tried my very best. We agreed, I would prep him – *you* would babysit him out there. I don't see what more we could have done. Let's just put it behind us and move on.

M.

From: Chris Whitty [mailto: cwhitty@gov.uk]
Sent: 3rd March 2020 18:33
To: M [mailto: m@axworthy.com]
Subject: Shaking Hands

M,

He said he went to a hospital with coronavirus patients and shook hands with everyone he met. He said that. He actually said that with his colourless lips. Did you make him say that? And if not, did he tell you he was *going* to say that?

Chris.

From: M [mailto: m@axworthy.com]
Sent: 3rd March 2020 18:36
To: Chris Whitty [mailto: cwhitty@gov.uk]
Subject: Shaking Hands

Chris,

Give me some credit. Of course I didn't make him say that. If I'd had any sort of inkling he was going to come out with that chuntering toffee, I would've filled his mouth with dry cream crackers and locked him in a cupboard.

Remember this is Boris Johnson we're talking about. Boris. Johnson. This is the sort of man we're dealing with now – someone who trots off to country retreats every weekend to argue with his girlfriend, who misses half a dozen COBRA meetings, who doesn't read anything he's given and who generally bumbles around Number 10 hoisting up his saggy trousers, burping in Latin and scratching his head in complete befuddlement over everything the job throws at him.

And yet he can slide into a daily briefing about something as serious as a global pandemic and boldly reel off several bubbles of unintelligible guff because his privileged background has given him the brass-balled confidence to do so. This is where we are now. This is it.

As I say, I tried my very best.

M.

From: Chris Whitty [mailto: cwhitty@gov.uk]
Sent: 3rd March 2020 18:51
To: M [mailto: m@axworthy.com]
Subject: Shaking Hands

M,

But we're the ones who are going to get it in the neck. Us. The experts. I'm the Chief Medical Officer for England FFS. The more they keep saying 'guided by the science', the more people are going to point the finger of blame at us. This virus is killing people around the world on a daily basis now and his top tip was to 'wash your hands with soap and hot water while singing "Happy Birthday" twice'. Mass gatherings should be banned, pubs and bars should be closed. Sod 'Happy Birthday'. He won't get fired for this kind of negligence, but we will.

Chris.

From: M [mailto: m@axworthy.com]
Sent: 3rd March 2020 18:59
To: Chris Whitty [mailto: cwhitty@gov.uk]
Subject: Shaking Hands

Chris,

You have my word that no scientist will be fired during this crisis. I know the govt's first priority is not to alarm people but if you have cold hard facts, as a scientist, it's your responsibility to deliver them. Whatever the useless bags of mince at the middle podium have to say every day, *you* must make sure the public are updated on the virus as accurately as possible.

If Matt Hancock or Boris Johnson say 'just get on with your daily life – you'll be fine as long as you belt out "Abide With Me" at the sink', then you have my authority to smack them down – figuratively and literally.

M.

From: Chris Whitty [mailto: cwhitty@gov.uk]
To: M [mailto: m@axworthy.com]
Sent: 3rd March 2020 19:05
Subject: Shaking Hands

Fine. But this is going to get a whole lot worse before it gets better.

From: M [mailto: m@axworthy.com]
Sent: 3rd March 2020 19:12
To: Chris Whitty [mailto: cwhitty@gov.uk]
Subject: Shaking Hands

Thanks, I'll find out what that is in Latin and tattoo it on Boris Johnson's forehead.

Diary: Monday 16th March 2020

First day of lockdown.

For most of the day, I sat in my study staring out of the window. I saw a van parked across the road advertising quartz worktops and after several hours concluded that their tagline should be 'don't take quartz for granite'. So a productive day, all in all.

Of course, I could be doing my job remotely. That's usually the only way I can do my job. But it's clear Axworthy have decided to furlough me to take me out of the firing line while these investigations into our organisation are still ongoing.

I can understand that. To be honest, I'm enjoying the time off. I'm pretending my house is a hotel that I've escaped to for a mini break. This morning for breakfast I imagined I was at a buffet by standing over the toaster with my plate in my hand. It's the little things.

I also decided to do the Joe Wicks school workout with the children. Every day he's going to livestream a workout from his YouTube channel. Highly commendable, of course, but I wonder how long he's going to keep it up for. If we're in this for the long haul, I fully expect him to lose it one morning and smash his mint green guitar against the fireplace (for 12 reps in 5 sets).

27th March

Dear Boris,

I don't understand. How did this happen? Apart from not attending COBRA meetings, not listening to the scientists, not following what other countries have done, not keeping yourself isolated, not wearing a face mask and visiting hospitals to shake hands with coronavirus patients, you did everything right.

I guess this is one for future historians to unpick!

Get well soon, M.

5 April 2020 13:05

Are you in the US yet?

> Being driven to the White House. This is madness. I was enjoying furlough at home. I really got into that daytime programme where dull couples buy dull houses in dull towns, what's it called? *Dull Dull Dull* or something.

What's on the agenda?

> Trump briefing at 5. According to intel, he's becoming more unhinged than normal. He's manipulating the coronavirus story to serve his own megalomaniac narrative, i.e. he is the hero of the hour, the man with the plan, the custodian of the cure. He knows this will go down well with his core support in the run up to the election this November. It's tinpot tyranny.

Well, let me know if you need any help.

I'm being driven to a building where they don't wear face masks or protective clothing but *do* have a big bowl of candy on the desk in reception. Of course I need help.

TRUMP'S DAILY BRIEFING SCRIPT – APRIL 5TH 2020

I'll put this to Anthony. When I closed the country to China, the China ban, whatever you want to call it, Anthony said I saved a lot of lives by doing that.

The hospital levels are starting to perhaps decrease.

We've also bought a tremendous amount of Hydroxychloroquine.

It's worked unbelievably. It's a powerful drug. And there are signs that it works on Covid-19.

It also works very powerfully on lupus.

And if you have no signs of heart problems, there's azithromycin, which will kill certain things that you don't want living.

You know the expression, I've used it for certain reasons, what do you have to lose? What do you have to lose?

I've seen things I sort of like but what do I know, I'm not a doctor.

M

Don't bring in Dr Fauci. When you mention Dr Fauci in your briefings, his squirming is audible.

M

Perhaps find out what it's called given that YOU imposed it.

M

Please leave Dr Fauci out of this. He's worn down. YOU'VE worn him down. And now he's just a pebble wearing a pair of glasses.

M

Perhaps decrease? This is supposed to be a briefing not a fortune cookie.

M

If you can say this without biting your tongue and falling over, I'll give you a dollar. Not that you should be mentioning unproven drugs whilst talking about coronavirus. People are scared. They want cures. But this isn't it. It's dangerous so don't mention it again.

M

Yes on malaria. Not coronavirus.

M

No there aren't, there isn't a single glimmer of a hope of a fart of a sign.

M

Yes and people suffering FROM lupus, can't GET their Hydroxychloroquine, because you keep telling people with coronavirus to take it, you stupid wet bag of sand.

M

Again, unproven and with dangerous side effects.

M

This is like listening to a pharmacist who's just bumped his head. You are not qualified to talk about this. You're not qualified to talk about anything this important. You shouldn't even be trusted with scissors.

M

Your hair. Your eyesight. Lots and lots of blood, there's three things.

M

Or a politician. Or a statesman. Or a responsible adult.

12 April 2020 20:01

Tell your boss to call me.

Mr Cummings is recuperating but I'm sure he'll make time for you soon, M.

Tell your boss to call me now.

Listen, your intimidation and insults don't work any more. The game is changing. Dominic will see you when he wants to see you.

The game is changing? You're not a protagonist in a John Grisham novel, you 14yo bogey, just fetch your master and bring him to me before I demote you so fast, you'll be back in reception class watching Hey Duggee.

To be honest, I'm surprised you're back on the scene. I hear the Telegraph are on the cusp of an exclusive about you and Axworthy!

You heard wrong. Due to the lockdown every newspaper's budget is being cut which means all costly investigations have been shut down. How do you like those sweet Braeburns, Milkybar Kid?

Be that as it may, your time is up. Westminster – and the White House for that matter – won't put up with you and your organisation's culture of bullying any more.

We are not bullies. We are advisers. That's what we do. If we appear forceful from time to time it's because you never take our BLOODY ADVICE. Now tell Cummings to call me and explain why, when he's supposed to be shielding in London, he decided to drive five hours to his parents' house in Durham this weekend. Because, trust me, he's going to need one hell of a water-tight story if this ever breaks out.

From: M [mailto: m@axworthy.com]
Sent: 24th April 2020 21:09
To: A [mailto: a@axworthy.com]
Subject: My Concerns (Part 217)

Dear A,

As usual, I have just been advising the President during his daily briefing and regret to inform you that I am through. I've had enough. No more. I can't do it.

Here are some quotes from the briefing.

'Supposing we hit the body with a tremendous er . . . whether it's ultraviolet or a just a very powerful light. And I think you said [to Dr Deborah Birx] that hasn't been checked but you're going to test it? And then I said supposing you brought the light inside the body, which you can do either through the skin or . . .'

'Right, and then I see the disinfectant where it knocks it out in a minute . . . one minute . . . and is there a way we can do something like that . . . by injection inside or . . . almost a cleaning . . . ? Because you see it gets on the lungs and does a tremendous number on the lungs so it'll be interesting to check that.'

From a purely selfish career-building point of view, I don't really want future leaders/clients to watch the President of the United States suggest his people inject themselves with bleach to cure Covid-19, and then wonder if it was *me* who told him to say that. He's destroying my reputation, frankly, and I cannot be part of this travelling circus any more.

I will continue to navigate Boris Johnson away from flying into the sun as normal but I must relinquish my duties to the White House as soon as possible.

You know, it's funny. Trump said to me once, 'You're a JOKE. You're THROUGH!' I never thought for a moment he could be right. But it turns out he was.

I guess that's just the way the world works now. Guys like him always end up being right, even when they're wrong.

Best,

M.

AXWORTHY GLO[BAL]

PO BOX 998 · ALDINGTON S[...]

From: M

To: PM Boris Johnson

Date: 27/04/2020

Heading: Project Second Chance

Message:

Believe it or not, while you were recuperating from coronavirus people didn't actively loathe you. There was actually a spot of sympathy for your situation. So it's time to build on that by hitting the ground running and tackling the items on this list, this week. Do you hear me? *This week.* That means working every day, 9–5, Monday to Friday. No excuses. Don't take Wednesday off and visit a crazy-golf course. Here you go:

1. Find the balance between lockdown measures to keep us all safe and supporting the economy. This does not mean relaxing measures to appease your billionaire friends such as that disgusting Wetherspoons grinch who looks like a festering radish exploding in a bowl of porridge.

2. Get an app designed that can test, track and trace anyone showing symptoms. Testing is frankly the priority right now. Actually, it should have been

Nikki – When the PM returns to full duties, make sure he reads this first. I don't care how you do it – staple it to his tie, pretend it's a list of single women in Camberwell, whatever – just make him read it. M.

the priority in January when you and the cabinet thought an extra couple of aloe vera pump bottles in the bathroom cabinet would shoo the virus away. Hey ho.

3. Tell Dominic Cummings that he can now only attend meetings given by the Scientific Advisory Group if he earns himself a qualification in science or medicine rather than simply continuing to be what he is – a piss-poor blogger. If he's going to keep rocking up to these meetings in his oversized jacket and woolly hat like a cocksure owl, perverting them with his own devious subplots, there's no point in the meetings even taking place. Tell him to stay at home.

4. Keir Starmer is not Jeremy Corbyn. At Prime Minister's Questions he'll be all over your errors of judgement like fucking Quincy, M.E. He knows we're falling behind the rest of the world and he's ready to pounce. So here are my five rules:

   a) Read my notes before all PMQs.
   b) Improve your delivery.
   c) Try as often as possible not to be you.
   d) Don't be funny – there are no sycophantic backbenchers to pretend to phwa-phwa at your tedious drivel as long as lockdown measures are in place.
   e) Try to actually answer some questions. That's what the Q stands for after all.

If you don't act now, you know what's going to happen. Starmer looks as hungry for power as Blair did. And I'm sorry but he looks more like a prime minister than you, too.

Whenever you're in the same room together it looks like a mortgage adviser posing with a scarecrow he's constructed from Weetabix.

AXWORTHY GLOBAL

PO BOX 998 · ALDINGTON ST · KW17 5EH

From: M

To: All @ DowningStComms

Date: 09/05/2020

Heading: Stay Home, Go Out, Save Lives?

Message:

What on God's Green Pancakes is this new slogan about?

From what I gather 'Stay Alert, Control the Virus, Save Lives' is a consciously underhanded shift away from the original central message of 'staying at home' because you want to kickstart the economy.

But because the virus is still causing hundreds of deaths a day, with no signs of slowing down, you've told people that staying home is still the best option. So in other words, stay in but go out. Perfect.

I don't recall Second World War posters adopting a similarly ambiguous tone.

'We Can Do It Maybe!'

'Dig For Victory If You Want, It's Up To You!'

'Careless Talk Costs Lives But Feel Free To Have A Natter With Your Neighbour I Suppose, Can't Do Any Harm Can It? Unless It Can. Perhaps It Can. Who Knows!'

In light of this new approach, how about this slogan to make it even clearer?

Stay alert

Have a barbecue

But make it a small one

Don't invite Geoff, he's got underlying health problems

Take him a plate of sausages or something later

And a beer

That's OK probably

Save lives

Let me know.

Best,

M.

AXWORTHY GLOBAL

PO BOX 998 · ALDINGTON ST · KW17 5EH

From: M

To: Dominic Cummings

Date: 25/05/2020

Heading: Notes ahead of briefing

Message:

Wow, it never rains but it shits, eh, Dom?

Some notes for you before you go into the lion's den. I know you probably don't want to read them because, to put no finer point on it, you can't bear me. But give it a quick once-over, it might save your career! Unless you want to go back to writing blog posts that no one reads. Up to you.

There will be times in this briefing when you'll feel as if you're being hung out to dry, which will at least get rid of some of your creases. However, follow my lead and you should be fine.

The journos are going to go hard on Barnard Castle and will ask why you broke lockdown guidelines to drive there. Here's Plan A:

Lie and blame your wife.

There is no Plan B.

If you make it as clear as you can (although admittedly it's going to be bloody difficult because your alibi makes about as much sense as a David Lynch film) that you drove to Barnard Castle to 'test your eyesight', then I can at least get a couple of spineless cabinet members to back up your story by saying they've done the same. I'll text Michael Gove and Matt Hancock: they'll do it. They're not called 'The Welcome Mat Twins' for nothing.

Remember not to use your favoured buzzword 'reasonable calculations'. I know you like to think you could win the public over if you got them to put themselves in your position and analyse the hard choices that you faced, but the fact is that tactic won't work. A single mother of three who's had no respite for months, who's worrying about money, who has not seen her elderly relatives since March, is not going to suddenly bolt upright on her sofa after watching you for 20 minutes and say, 'My God, those *were* reasonable calculations! I've been wrong about this all along. In many ways he's actually a hero!' You were perceived as a villain before this and you will be perceived as a villain after. This is just damage limitation.

Don't use your blog about the coronavirus from last year to prove you are knowledgeable on the subject. If you do, I guarantee at least one journalist will do the research and discover you edited that blog a few weeks ago to include the reference to coronavirus. Every edit and every update made on a blog is recorded. It won't take a cyber-genius to discover your cack-handed tinkering. Remember you are a conman, a caricature, a sidekick to a comic book villain, a walking laundry basket of soiled jeans. You are *not* a Svengali and you never will be.

Hope that's helped!

Looking forward to seeing you at the bottom of the rose garden like a terrified gnome.

Best of luck,

M.

Diary: Wednesday 27th May 2020

Furloughed again. Cummings is behind it this time. Def.

To be honest, I was finding it hard to keep up with this government. I mean, even a shitshow needs an interval.

This evening I was contacted by the journalist at the 'Telegraph' who was going to do the big exposé on Axworthy – and me. It seems they used the virus as an excuse for the article to be unceremoniously dropped. One of those happy coincidences. Took her years to write, apparently. I told her to keep her research for a rainy day. She said, 'Everything has gone already,' and hung up.

I guess I should never have worried. Friends in high places and all that.

Maybe I'll pen my own exposé. At least then I can be sure that the last four years weren't a fever dream.

Right, got to go. My children need some more expert home tuition. I've got a business class prepared for them entitled 'Paw Patrol: A lesson in regional budgets and overspending'.

They need to know the truth.

Diary: Thursday 2nd July 2020

Back from my latest furlough. I'm in and out more often than a meerkat.

'We don't need you at this current moment in time.' Until yesterday this was the official line from Keir Starmer's people. So we just waited. Because eventually they all need us.

'The Black Lives Matter moment' he called it. Not movement. Moment. All because this talk about defunding the police has given him the needle.

You could tell in the interview that Sir Keir was irritated, probably the spikiest I've ever seen him. Usually he's such a relaxed soul, often looking like that chilled businessman on holiday in Tuscany that you get quite pally with by the pool. As a former Director of Public Prosecutions, though, he was bristling at the very suggestion of reducing police budgets. Hence 'moment'. Silly boy. Just goes to show that even the smoothest operator can get his braces in a twist and require our assistance.

So anyway, that's looking like the next project – along with the continued inept handling of the coronavirus pandemic by this wagon of shame otherwise known as Her Majesty's Government.

The latest shambolic, clear-as-a-horse's-arse directive is the wearing of face masks. First of all they say face masks should be mandatory on public transport but optional in bars, restaurants and shops. Then they say hold on, sorry, it should be mandatory in bars, restaurants and shops. Then some ministers approach me on the quiet and voice their concern that the enforced wearing of masks will enrage their core voters, who somehow equate wearing a bit of fabric to stop them dying as some sort of Orwellian free speech muzzle.

So now we're talking about face masks being optional if you're only 'popping in' to a bar, restaurant or shop. I mean, it's politics on amphetamines.

And let's not forget that all these instructions are occurring FOUR MONTHS TOO LATE. Why are we debating face masks now? Presumably a big announcement is on the cards regarding the closing of stable doors following a big spike last month in bolted horses.

I just wish there was some kind of an end to all this. A new story rather than a depressing continuation of the same old tired mulch.

But that's what I'm here for. To try and change it. To steer things in a different direction. To introduce a new narrative. And I guess it would be remiss of me to chuck it all in now when the work's not finished.

Just received three garbled text messages from the PM. He does tend to suffer from frantic thumb syndrome when he's nervous. Not even autocorrect knows what he's on about. His muddled sentences look like dubious links to Bitcoin sites.

Better text him back or he'll get worried and start pacing the corridors, which, when you've got the posture and grace of a panda with shoeboxes on its feet, doesn't inspire confidence in your colleagues.

Oh, well. Another day in this never-ending hellscape. Onwards.